BOOK OF SECRETS

C HKPG KH UGETGVKXG DQQM

The code is on page 8

BOOK OF SECRETS

Andrews McMeel Publishing

Kansas City

BOOK OF SECRETS

For information, write to Andrews McMeel Publishing, an Andrews McMeel Universal company, 4520 Main Street, Kansas City, Missouri 64111.

ISBN-13: 978-0-7407-5561-3
ISBN-10: 0-7407-5561-7

Library of Congress Control Number: 2005929263

05 06 07 08 09 IMA 10 9 8 7 6 5 4 3 2 1

Produced by Essential Works
168a Camden Street, London, NW1 9PT, England

Designed by Kate Ward for Essential Works

Images of abandoned New York subway stations courtesy of Joseph Brennan

INTRODUCTION

KNOWLEDGE IS POWER.

Of course, power corrupts, but who doesn't want to be corrupted a little? Who doesn't want to know as much as possible about everything and anything? Clearly you do, or you wouldn't be reading this book. It's a strange thing, but the world is becoming ever more public, in as much as there are cameras watching our every move, and electronic tracking devices that can pinpoint what we have spent where and when. The notion of "private lives" is a quaint anachronism, and yet the world is still full of secrets. Those secrets can be big or small, white or very dark, but they are all the currency of people who like to deal in knowledge. Or rather, hold back their secret knowledge because it can make them richer—monetarily or spiritually. In an age when man is constantly bombarded with information from all manner of media, including 24-hour news broadcasts, internet streaming and mobile telecommunications technology, that secrets exist is in itself an amazing fact.

The quest to uncover secrets has driven men to madness and great feats of discovery, it has brought them to ruin and great riches—Colonel Sanders, for instance, would never have created the KFC empire without the secret element in his Southern fried chicken. Similarly, Coca-Cola would be just another soft drink without its secret ingredient. Then there are the worlds' secret services, who have made and prevented wars by their very secret activities.

This book is too small to contain all of the secrets of the world, of course. Any book would be too small, but it does contain an incredible array of secrets, from an impressive range of subject areas. There are food secrets, secret buildings, secrets of the rich and famous, secrets of success and of human relationships plus many more. You can dip in and out and absorb the secrets contained within these pages, and so feel a little wiser and a little more knowledgeable. Go on, corrupt yourself a little.

X (editor)

THE SECRET OF ATTRACTING BEAUTIFUL WOMEN

According to legend, Freud's dying words were: "What do women want?" Thankfully for men, post-Freud teachings have produced a glut of soul-searching self-help books that reveal just that. In no particular order, here are the top ten things women secretly look for in a man.

1. BE APPEALING.

After first impressions have faded, women are more attracted to a man's manner than his look. A man should therefore work on honing his charm and becoming more appealing. Looks aren't everything.

2. LEAD AN INTERESTING LIFE.

A recent survey revealed that more than anything else, women look for a man who has led an interesting life, citing their ideal men as Bill Clinton, Sting, and even Prince Charles. So don't refer to your failed business venture; instead, spin the truth to make the episode sound like yet another example of your brave, impetuous, go-getting nature.

3. AIM HIGHER.

Beautiful women frequently complain that men never approach them. This is because male pride doesn't take well to rejection. But if you become the kind of a man who can approach these women, you may be surprised by the success you have. Remember: men who are successful with women are merely those who have experienced more rejection.

4. DRESS WELL.

Women like a man who is well groomed and tidy. Or, in other words, one who is presentable in public. But don't spend too much time on your appearance—a woman will rarely date a man who is prettier than she is.

5. MAKE HER LAUGH.

Woody Allen often jokes that he has never laughed a woman into bed, yet he has been surprisingly successful with women. Plus, a GSOH (Good Sense Of Humor) is still the most popular phrase in personal ads. A woman will find humor entertaining, of course, and a sure-fire guarantee of no awkward silences on a date. This subconsciously means that she can relax and be the passenger, not the driver.

6. BE SINCERE.

Women are receptive to men who are kind, thoughtful, sincere, and good listeners.

7. BUT DON'T BE TOO SINCERE.

Another study revealed that women instinctively divide men into those they consider friends, and those who have the potential to become lovers. The sweet man will only ever be the friend.

8. PLAY CAT AND MOUSE.

If she's playing hard to get, then do the same—over-eager men, like over-eager women, can appear desperate. But you must make the next move. A woman never wants to feel like the predator.

9. MAKE HER FEEL SPECIAL.

Treat her as if she's unique, unlike anyone else you have ever met. Appreciate her and never take her for granted.

10. DO YOUR HOMEWORK.

Find out what her father is like—for most women, he will be the first and most powerful image of manhood. Then determine what you want: women want a fling with a cad but a relationship with a dad. Manipulate your game plan accordingly. ❀

THE SECRET GERMAN LINK BETWEEN ELVIS, FRANK SINATRA, AND THE BEATLES

German orchestra leader Bert Kaempfert is the only man to ever link the towering figures of popular music Elvis Presley, The Beatles, and Frank Sinatra. In 1961, in Hamburg, it was Kaempfert who invited The Beatles to make their first visit to a professional recording studio, where the group recorded "My Bonnie." The Liverpool teenagers were particularly impressed to find out that Kaempfert was the man who had written "Wooden Heart" for Elvis. A few years later, Kaempfert made it a hat-trick when he wrote Frank Sinatra's only #1 of the rock 'n' roll era, 1966's "Strangers In The Night." While "My Bonnie" was musically unremarkable, its lasting place in Beatle history lies in the fact that it was the record which was to alert Brian Epstein to the existence of the band.

A	B	C	D	E	F	G	H	I	J	K	L	M	N	O	P	Q	R	S	T	U	V	W	X	Y	Z
B	C	D	E	F	G	H	I	J	K	L	M	N	O	P	Q	R	S	T	U	V	W	X	Y	Z	A
C	D	E	F	G	H	I	J	K	L	M	N	O	P	Q	R	S	T	U	V	W	X	Y	Z	A	B
D	E	F	G	H	I	J	K	L	M	N	O	P	Q	R	S	T	U	V	W	X	Y	Z	A	B	C
E	F	G	H	I	J	K	L	M	N	O	P	Q	R	S	T	U	V	W	X	Y	Z	A	B	C	D
F	G	H	I	J	K	L	M	N	O	P	Q	R	S	T	U	V	W	X	Y	Z	A	B	C	D	E
G	H	I	J	K	L	M	N	O	P	Q	R	S	T	U	V	W	X	Y	Z	A	B	C	D	E	F
H	I	J	K	L	M	N	O	P	Q	R	S	T	U	V	W	X	Y	Z	A	B	C	D	E	F	G
I	J	K	L	M	N	O	P	Q	R	S	T	U	V	W	X	Y	Z	A	B	C	D	E	F	G	H
J	K	L	M	N	O	P	Q	R	S	T	U	V	W	X	Y	Z	A	B	C	D	E	F	G	H	I
K	L	M	N	O	P	Q	R	S	T	U	V	W	X	Y	Z	A	B	C	D	E	F	G	H	I	J
L	M	N	O	P	Q	R	S	T	U	V	W	X	Y	Z	A	B	C	D	E	F	G	H	I	J	K
M	N	O	P	Q	R	S	T	U	V	W	X	Y	Z	A	B	C	D	E	F	G	H	I	J	K	L
N	O	P	Q	R	S	T	U	V	W	X	Y	Z	A	B	C	D	E	F	G	H	I	J	K	L	M
O	P	Q	R	S	T	U	V	W	X	Y	Z	A	B	C	D	E	F	G	H	I	J	K	L	M	N
P	Q	R	S	T	U	V	W	X	Y	Z	A	B	C	D	E	F	G	H	I	J	K	L	M	N	O
Q	R	S	T	U	V	W	X	Y	Z	A	B	C	D	E	F	G	H	I	J	K	L	M	N	O	P
R	S	T	U	V	W	X	Y	Z	A	B	C	D	E	F	G	H	I	J	K	L	M	N	O	P	Q
S	T	U	V	W	X	Y	Z	A	B	C	D	E	F	G	H	I	J	K	L	M	N	O	P	Q	R
T	U	V	W	X	Y	Z	A	B	C	D	E	F	G	H	I	J	K	L	M	N	O	P	Q	R	S
U	V	W	X	Y	Z	A	B	C	D	E	F	G	H	I	J	K	L	M	N	O	P	Q	R	S	T
V	W	X	Y	Z	A	B	C	D	E	F	G	H	I	J	K	L	M	N	O	P	Q	R	S	T	U
W	X	Y	Z	A	B	C	D	E	F	G	H	I	J	K	L	M	N	O	P	Q	R	S	T	U	V
X	Y	Z	A	B	C	D	E	F	G	H	I	J	K	L	M	N	O	P	Q	R	S	T	U	V	W
Y	Z	A	B	C	D	E	F	G	H	I	J	K	L	M	N	O	P	Q	R	S	T	U	V	W	X
Z	A	B	C	D	E	F	G	H	I	J	K	L	M	N	O	P	Q	R	S	T	U	V	W	X	Y

ABANDONED NEW YORK SUBWAY STATIONS #1

CITY HALL

LOCATION: UNDER CITY HALL PARK

OPENED IN OCTOBER 1904, CLOSED IN DECEMBER 1945.

It was the original southern terminal of the Interborough Rapid Transit (IRT) subway and designed to be the showpiece of the new subway. Unusually elegant in architectural style, it is unique among the original IRT stations in that the platform and mezzanine feature Guastavino arches and skylights, colored glass tilework, and brass chandeliers. Because its platform is short and very tightly curved, when increased ridership of the subway required that original 5-car local stations be lengthened to accommodate longer trains, it was abandoned in favor of the nearby Brooklyn Bridge station. While very few people have actually seen City Hall Station, the #6 train still passes through it on its way northbound, reversing direction using the loop for the journey back to the Bronx. On the surface, all that can be seen of the station is a concrete slab inset with glass tiles, which are the skylights for the platform below. This patch of concrete is in the middle of a grove of dogwoods in front of City Hall, close to Broadway. Recent security measures at City Hall have closed the area to visitors.

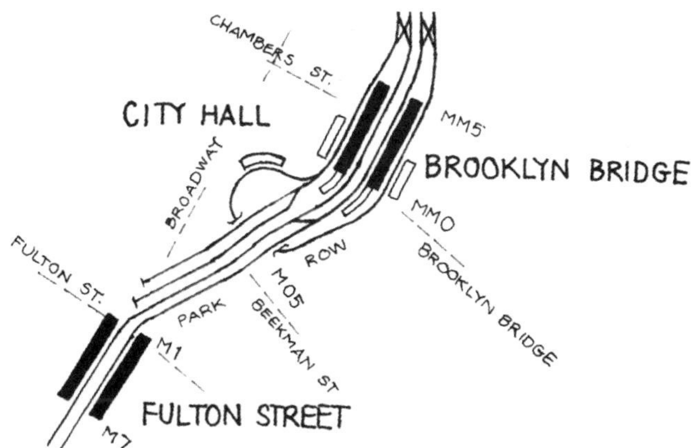

Opposite: The Vigenere Cipher, used by the Confederate Army.

THE SECRET TO SURVIVING A SHARK ATTACK

The best way to survive the attack of a shark is to avoid it. So don't swim in any waters where sharks are likely to also swim and certainly don't swim where there's low visibility and/or no lifeguard on duty. Also remember that sharks feed at night.

If you must swim where sharks are known to exist, don't swim alone. Do not wear bright colors in the water. The kind of food that sharks are attracted to tends to be silver, white, or yellow, so don't wear jewelry either, since that can have the same reflective effect and attract sharks. Don't swim in commercial fishing areas. If you spot shoals of small, silver fish in the water, there are likely to be sharks watching the same shoal. Likewise, the presence of birds in the water or swooping into it is a sign that the shark's favorite food is around. Sharks have a highly developed sense of smell and can detect blood and waste matter from miles away. Don't swim if you're bleeding, and definitely do not pass body waste into the water. Even if you spot a shark nearby, control your bodily functions.

If you are attacked by a shark, make a lot of noise and splash heavily. Some authorities recommend shouting under water. Despite what you might think, lying "dead" in the water will attract a shark to bite you. Swim fast and messily and change direction suddenly—sharks are like tankers in that they can't change direction as quickly as they'd like (which is why dolphins often get the better of them). If you're with people, bunch together and all kick or punch at the approaching shark. If you have a knife on you, aim it at the shark's eyes or gills. Of course, because none of us ever has the sharp knife we need when we need it, you can punch or gouge at the shark's eyes—that is, if you have the nerve to face it. Swimming away from the shark is the best course of action, even if you've been bitten.

Whatever happens, keep moving, making a noise, and try to attract the attention of others—and never, ever, give up.

A PRESIDENT SPEAKS ON SECRETS

"THE VERY WORD 'SECRECY' IS REPUGNANT IN A FREE AND OPEN SOCIETY; AND WE ARE AS A PEOPLE INHERENTLY AND HISTORICALLY OPPOSED TO SECRET SOCIETIES, TO SECRET OATHS, AND TO SECRET PROCEEDINGS."

John F. Kennedy (*member of the Ancient Order of Hibernians 1947–1963, U.S. president 1961–1963*)

THE CATERPILLAR SNAKE'S SURVIVAL SECRET

The caterpillar of the tiger swallowtail butterfly is fat, luscious, and juicy, an appetizing little hors d'oeuvre for any gourmet bird. However, it has two bright yellow markings on its rear end that make it look like the head of a snake, which would certainly not find its way onto any bird's menu. The tiger swallowtail butterfly is absolutely determined to get a good start in life. In addition to having a well-camouflaged caterpillar, its larva looks exactly like a bird dropping. Which is pretty off-putting, even for the hungriest predator.

LITTLE KNOWN CULINARY CURIOS #1

Freshly killed chickens will always have more flavor. They can be bought at kosher shops.

It takes almost five kilos of grapes to produce one kilo of raisins, sultanas, or currants.

Stir a teaspoon of cornflour mixed into a paste with water into yogurt before adding to a sauce as a healthy substitute for cream. It will stop it separating when it gets hot.

Adding salt to dried beans' cooking water will toughen the bean skins.

WHY A CRASHED COMET LEAVES NO CRATER

When, on 30 June, 1908, a mysterious explosion flattened around half a million acres of forest near the Podkamennay Tunguska River in central Siberia, Russia, the blast could be heard up to 500 miles away and eyewitnesses reported seeing a shining object in the sky, moving toward the earth. What caused the explosion and why were particles of extra-terrestrial magnetite and silicate found in the soil and embedded in trees nearby? In the 1920s, Soviet scientist Leonid Kulik thought the cataclysm was due to a meteorite, but was puzzled that there was no crater or rock fragments around. His investigative myopia prevented him from understanding the secret cause of the explosion: a collision of a fragment of comet with the Earth. A comet, a "dirty snowball" comprised of ice and dust, had vaporized a few miles above the taiga, creating a fireball and ballistic wave. It weighed hundreds of thousands of tons and would have been traveling at around 60,000 miles per hour. The resulting explosion was equivalent to between 10 and 15 megatons of TNT, nearly 1,000 times more powerful than the first atomic bombs.

THE SECRETS OF GIVING FLOWERS #1

In the restrained, subtle Victorian era, when actions spoke louder than words and much was left unsaid, seduction was highly codified and the giving of flowers was particularly symbolic. The giving of flowers is a much more complicated business than one might think. The various meanings of individual flowers are not always favorable or even consistent with each other, and there are secret messages to be found in how they are presented:

With blooms facing upwards
my message is favorable

With blooms facing downwards
my message is unfavorable

Given with the right hand
I agree

Flowers given with the left hand
I disagree

Kissing a received flower
yes

Plucking or discarding a petal
no

SECRETS OF YOUR COMPUTER KEYBOARD

AOL's keyboard grime analysis established that the major constituents of a London office's keyboard dirt are as follows:

Item	%
Corn Flakes	15%
Hard candy	15%
Noodles	7%
Vegetable piece	4%
Leaf	1%
Pencil lead/shavings	1%
Staple	1%
Finger nail	1%
Tape/plastic	1%
Insect	1%
Foil	1%
Hair	1%

THE SECRET BERLIN TUNNEL

During the Cold War Berlin held many secrets and the Altglienicke district of the city was the site of one of the most audacious intelligence coups of the era. Starting in 1954, a 500-meter tunnel was constructed from West to East Berlin in order to intercept landlines used by Soviet military and intelligence. Unknown to the CIA, however, the entire operation had been compromised by a British mole, George Blake. The construction of the tunnel was allowed to continue though, as his handler didn't want to run the risk of exposing their star agent. Initially, the KGB kept knowledge of the tunnel from the GRU (Soviet Military Intelligence) and their East German allies. The tunnel was eventually "accidentally" discovered in April 1956, but not before the operation had produced some 50,000 reels of magnetic tapes of Soviet and East German telephone and teletype traffic. The western intelligence agencies were still interpreting this information more than two years after the closure of the tunnel.

This was not the only Cold War-era tunnel dug in Berlin, though. On 14 September 1962, 29 people fled under the Berlin Wall through a 126-meter tunnel that ran from an East German cellar into the Western zone. Flooding shortly afterwards prevented any others from using the same method of escape.

THE SORCERER WHO INSPIRED HARRY POTTER

From where does J. K. Rowling get her inspiration? History, it seems. The character of the sorcerer Nicolas Flamel, who appeared in the book *Harry Potter and the Sorcerer's Stone,* was based on a real medieval Parisian bookseller and alchemist. Born around 1330, Flamel spent much of his life searching for the "philosopher's stone," the substance that would turn base metals into gold and produce the elixir of life. After a premonition in a dream, he purchased a manuscript, *The Book of Abraham the Jew*, which he claimed contained the secrets of alchemy. The house in which Flamel lived at 51 Rue Montmorency in Paris is now a restaurant.

SECRETS OF THE HOUSE

1 A Casino speeds up the game if they are worried about losing money. On average, the more games played, the higher their percentage.
2 Are all the players genuine? People from outside, even security guards may be asked to play to make a Casino look fuller.
3 Casinos want you to lose touch with the outside world and your sense of time. There are no clocks inside a casino, croupiers do not wear watches, and often there are no windows.
4 Don't be pleasantly surprised by all the free drinks on offer in a casino. It's a business. They want to keep you there and the more drunk you are the less you're likely to win.
5 In a busy game, watch out for the guy who is prepared to steal chips from someone else's pile.

THE SECRET OF THE BLACK BOX?

Everyone knows that Black Box Flight Recorders aren't black—they're orange so as to be as conspicuous as possible. So why is it called that? Because the first version of the in-flight recorder was invented by a man named Black.

While originally they recorded everything that was said in the cabin, now they also keep a video record and monitor all the plane's operational systems.

HOW A NUCLEAR BOMB WORKS

DO NOT TELL ANYONE THIS.

There are two sorts of atomic explosion, those caused by nuclear fission and those caused by nuclear fusion. Each involves altering the amount of matter contained in atoms to reduce their mass and create the energy that manifests itself as a huge explosion. The former splits atoms to create two new ones from each, the total mass of which will be less than the original atom; fusion will join two atoms together to result in one single new atom that will be less than the original two. It's the difference in mass between what you started with and what you end up with that is converted into the energy that creates the explosion.

The chain reaction that occurs to give a nuclear bomb its power happens in a fission explosion when the atoms of an unstable "fissile" material—uranium, which consist of protons, neutrons, and electrons—are bombarded with extra neutrons, and split to release free neutrons of their own, which in turn cannon into other atoms in the uranium. The energy released as this happens is enormous.

A nuclear fusion explosion creates an even greater energy surge than fission, but for a long time was harder to achieve. It uses hydrogen not uranium (this is why some atomic bombs are referred to as hydrogen bombs) and fuses together two of the different atoms that make up the gas to create one single atom. Because these atoms, deuterium and tritium, naturally repel each other, they have to be heated to a temperature of over a million degrees centigrade before they fuse. But once that temperature is reached the fusion takes place in all the atoms at once, creating an explosion of energy. In power stations, lasers are fired at pellets of extracted deuterium and tritium, but in a fusion bomb, a small fission device will be used as the trigger to create the required temperature for fusion to occur.

UNDERGROUND SECRETS OF NEW YORK

In the 1980s a very secret, underground society sprang up under the Big Apple's streets, fuelled by poverty, homelessness, and drug addiction. The so-called Molemen lived in the vast network of tunnels beneath the city, with the total numbers estimated between 1,000 and 5,000. Many congregated in the area underneath Grand Central Station. Lurid reports were told of mutants or Chuds (Cannibalistic Humanoid Underground Dwellers), but the truth was sadder and more prosaic. Today, due to tougher law enforcement and outreach programs, there are fewer of them, but the secret Molemen of New York still exist.

WHEN REX ALMOST BECAME CARY

No one who has seen the movie *My Fair Lady* can possibly imagine anyone else in the role of Professor Henry Higgins. And yet, if it hadn't been for Cary Grant, Rex Harrison would not have won the role. Despite his having first played Higgins on Broadway in 1956, the movie's producer Jack Warner wasn't convinced that Harrison should have the film role. He toyed first with the idea of Noel Coward, Ray Milland, or Michael Redgrave playing Higgins, then newcomer Peter O'Toole caught his eye, and finally Warner became determined to cast Cary Grant as the singing professor. However, the artist formerly known as Archie Leach cabled back a response which was direct and unequivocal: "Not only will I not play Higgins, if you don't cast Rex Harrison, I won't go and *see* it!"

Although Harrison was concerned about his lack of a singing voice and consequently suffered terrible bouts of nerves, he had magnificently overcome his shortcomings on stage. One night, Spencer Tracy was in the audience with Frank Sinatra and backstage afterwards he gleefully told the British actor: "When you did that last number ["I've Grown Accustomed To Her Face"], you made the little wop cry!"

HOW THE KGB PASSED SECRETS IN THE WEST

The Russians always demonstrated a sense of humor when it came to espionage and operations on enemy soil. Since they were firmly against both organized religion and the trappings of capitalist success, KGB spymasters obviously thought that it would be amusing—and perhaps less suspicious—if they used churches in wealthy London areas for some of their dirty work. During the Cold War, the KGB operated two "dead letter drops" where agents left secret material to be picked up by their handlers in Kensington. One was behind two pillars near the Pieta statue in Brompton Oratory, a Catholic Church on the Brompton Road. Another was in the yard of Holy Trinity Church in Cottage Place, where packages were left by the tree beside a statue of St. Francis of Assisi.

SECRET TRICKS OF THE TRADE

ACTOR

A wise older actor once told Michael Caine, "don't act like a drunk man. Act like a drunk man trying hard to be sober."

GRAPHIC DESIGNER

To pacify the client who thinks they are a designer and cannot pass anything without making their mark, give your design an obvious mistake: a huge logo or dumb font. The client will correct that and your design will go through as it should.

BALLOON TWISTER

Don't specify in advance what animal you're making—you're setting yourself up for failure. Ask children afterwards what it looks like to them. Rely on their imagination.

MAKE-UP ARTIST

Applying a thin line of concealer around the outside edge of the lips gives them more definition. Dabbing lipgloss along the length of cheekbones makes them more prominent.

HAIRDRESSER

Watch your hairdresser's facial twitches and shoulder hunches in the mirror. Hairdressers utilize the complicated arrangements of mirrors in their salon to convey to each other urgent judgments about their clients.

SECRETS OF ALCHEMY

Alchemy is the speculative medieval science that tried to achieve the transmutation of base metals into gold—the process known as aurifaction. It also encompassed the quest for inner health and immortality. It was thought that by ingesting alchemical solutions and practicing morality, men could live forever.

※ ※ ※

The word alchemy was taken from the Arabic "al-kimiya," which encompassed both chemistry and alchemy—in practice, alchemists were creating chemical experiments by mixing various elements together in various procedures.

※ ※ ※

In the Middle Ages, alchemists revered the legendary Hermes Trismegistos ("thrice greatest Hermes," the name the Greeks gave to the Egyptian god Thoth) as the supposed founding genius of their science. The so-called Hermetic writings were in Greek and Latin and covered a range of occult and philosophical subjects. Thought to date from the first century A.D., they were the core texts of alchemical speculation. Hermes was also believed to be the author of a long-lost emerald tablet, on which the secret of the "grand arcanum" or philosopher's stone was inscribed.

※ ※ ※

Alchemy was closely linked to the study of astrology. It was thought that the seven principal metals developed within the earth, under the influence of the then (known) planets. The relationships were as follows: gold—Sun; silver—Moon; mercury—Mercury; copper—Venus; iron—Mars; tin—Jupiter; lead—Saturn.

※ ※ ※

Experimental by nature, the practice of alchemy varied, although a laboratory would usually contain certain key elements: a fire, mixing and measuring equipment, and apparatus for distillation.

※ ※ ※

Alchemy was regarded as a pursuit worthy of the finest minds. Roger Bacon, the 13th-century English monastic philosopher and scientist, believed that transmutation of gold was possible, although his own experiments came to nothing. The works attributed to Jabir ibn Hayyan, known in the West as Geber, were a 8th to 10th centuries collection of many Arabic works that helped make alchemy intellectually respectable in Europe. Albertus Magnus, the Dominican bishop and teacher of St. Thomas Aquinas, doubted the claims of alchemy, but nevertheless found his name attached to a curious legend. It was claimed that he administered an "elixir of life" to a statue, which then came to life and acted as his servant.

※ ※ ※

Central to the practice of alchemy was the legendary "philosopher's stone," described by Zosimus of Panopolis in around A.D. 300 as "the stone that is not a stone." This elusive substance was the agent by which base metals could be transmuted into gold. In the early 16th century, King James IV of Scotland employed a surgeon called John Damian to lead the search for it. He was appointed Abbot of Tongland, Galloway, and generously funded in his experiments. He failed in this endeavor, as he did in his near-fatal attempt in 1507 to fly from the ramparts of Stirling Castle. His leg broken, Damian blamed his plunge to the ground on his use of hen, rather than eagle, feathers.

※ ※ ※

In England, the mathematician and occultist John Dee advised both Queen Mary I and her successor Elizabeth I on astrology. Granted a license to practice alchemy, his laboratory was destroyed by a mob that feared he was dabbling in witchcraft.

※ ※ ※

The most celebrated alchemical treatise from the early modern period is the *Mutus Liber* (Wordless Book), first published in 1677 in France. It purported to be a guide to manufacturing the philosopher's stone, communicated through 15 mysterious images. The Latin inscription on the first plate claims that the book sets forth the whole of Hermetic philosophy.

※ ※ ※

The 17th-century natural philosopher Robert Boyle was an advocate of alchemy and successfully lobbied for the repeal of a 280-year-old law against "multiplying gold." Even in the age of scientific enlightenment, the lure of alchemy proved enduring. In 1782, the chemist James Price, a member of the renowned Royal Society, announced that he had created gold from base metals. He later committed suicide after the Society's president, Joseph Banks, challenged him to produce evidence to support his claims.

DISTINGUISHED GERMAN SECRETS

"WHOEVER WISHES TO KEEP A SECRET MUST HIDE THE FACT THAT HE POSSESSES ONE."
Johann Wolfgang von Goethe (*18th-century German poet and philosopher*)

"THE SECRET OF POLITICS? MAKE A GOOD TREATY WITH RUSSIA."
Otto von Bismarck (*19th-century founder of the German Empire*)

THE SECRET HISTORY OF KOTEX

Many technological innovations are developed during wartime. In 1914, the paper supplier Kimberly-Clark developed a new type of material out of processed wood and called it Cellucotton. It was half as cheap to produce as cotton and five times more absorbent. In a patriotic gesture it was soon being sold to the War Department at cost, and used to dress wounds in World War I.

When the war was over, the company had to find another use for its product. Until then, women had been using rags for sanitary protection, but someone came up with the idea of using Cellucotton for the same purpose. Their marketing agency suggested the name Kotex, an abbreviation of "cotton textile," and a whole new era of disposable sanitary products began.

In 1928, Lee Miller's image was one of the first to be used in a Kotex advertisement to her initial chagrin and later pride. Then magazines and retail outlets underwent a similar change of heart. To start with neither would take the products, but by 1935 Tampax had come on to the market and by 1945, American women were almost exclusively using commercially produced sanitary napkins and tampons. ⌛

THE SECRET TO SURVIVING SNAKE BITE

A lot of people get bitten by snakes in America—up to 50,000 a year, in fact. The secret to surviving a snake bite is primarily not to panic. Only a fifth of bites come from poisonous snakes and a ridiculously low number ever result in death (about 15 a year). So STAY CALM.

If bitten, sit still for half an hour or so. Any movement speeds up your blood flow (as does panicking, remember) and you don't want that. Get into a position that keeps the bitten area below heart level. Now remove anything that can impede blood flow, including rings, which will prevent the bite area from swelling. If the area of the bite begins to swell and change color, the snake was probably poisonous. That might put you into shock, so make sure that you're comfortable and able to keep warm.

If your bite is on a hand, finger, foot, or toe, wrap your leg or arm with a bandage (rip it from your clothes if necessary) and tie it between the bite and your heart, kind of like those ties that nurses put on when you're having a blood test. Try to leave any fang marks open to the air and make sure that the bandage allows flow of blood, only restricted.

Despite what you might have seen in the movies, do not either cut into the bite nor attempt to suck out the poison. And even if you could, don't put an ice pack or similar aide on the bite since that can make it worse.

Remain calm and after your half-hour rest walk steadily and at a not-too-fast pace to the nearest emergency room.

THE SECRET OF KEEPING BABIES QUIET

A reliable remedy for colic in babies is a teaspoon of onion water. Make an infusion by steeping a roughly chopped onion in hot water then leaving it to cool. This can be kept in a sealed jar, in the fridge, for three or four days.

ABANDONED NEW YORK SUBWAY STATIONS #2

COURT STREET

LOCATION: COURT STREET AT BOERUM PLACE AND SCHERMERHORN STREET

OPENED IN APRIL 1936, CLOSED JUNE 1946.

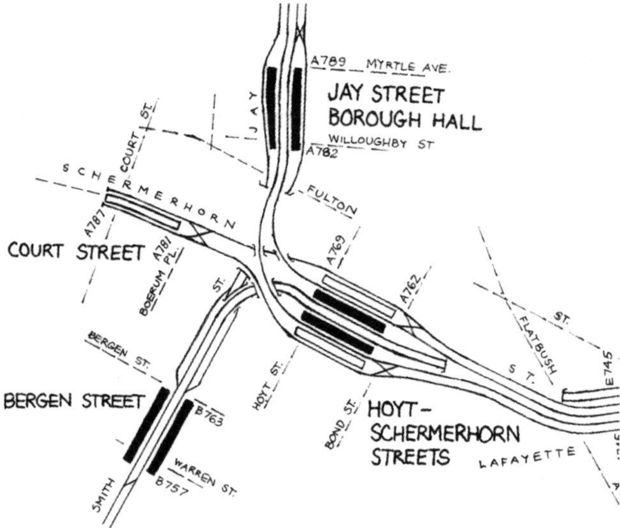

Because it is so close to stations with direct service to Manhattan, it never had much ridership. Its closure also eliminated any use for outer platforms at the nearby Hoyt-Schermerhorn Sts. Though almost unused for thirty years, in the 1960s it became a subway station set for movies, and an entrance at Boerum Place was reopened. It was perfect because trains could be put in it, and moved in and out as required for movie scenes, with no interference at all to regular train service. As part of their Bicentennial celebrations in 1976, the Transit Authority set up what was called the New York City Transit Exhibit at Court Street, which opened on July 4. Admission was one subway token. Although billed as temporary, it has continued to the present day, and is now known as the New York Transit Museum. Special *Nostalgia Train* tours operate in and out of the station a few times a year.

THE SECRET LANGUAGE OF CODE TALKERS

One of the stranger episodes in the secret history of cryptology was the use of Navajo speakers in the Second World War. The U.S. military, concerned over Japanese success in deciphering their codes, recruited a group of young Navajos and asked them to devise their own code. Everyday Navajo words were used to represent a military vocabulary—ships were named after fish, bombs were eggs and tanks were turtles. The Navajos found it ironic that their language was being enlisted for the service of the nation. At school, they had often been punished for speaking it. The code could be quickly transmitted and was never broken by the Japanese. The finest hour of the code talkers was at the bloody capture of Iwo Jima, where six Navajos transmitted more than 800 faultless messages.

THE SECRET OF GETTING RICE RIGHT #1

Wild rice isn't rice at all, but derives from a grass grown in water.

Wild rice is far more nutritious than the regular variety: it is rich in all eight amino acids, is much higher in fiber, lower in calories, and has hardly any gluten content.

You can reduce the cooking time of wild rice—about 60 minutes, twice that of regular rice—by soaking it overnight.

Stop rice sticking together by washing it under cold running water until the water runs clear before you start boiling it. This gets rid of the excess starch that causes the stickiness.

Do not stir rice while you are cooking it as this will release starch from the grains, which will stick them together.

Brown rice will take longer to cook than white rice—about 10 minutes longer—but brown rice will be chewier when cooked, so don't be tempted to overcook it thinking it isn't quite done yet.

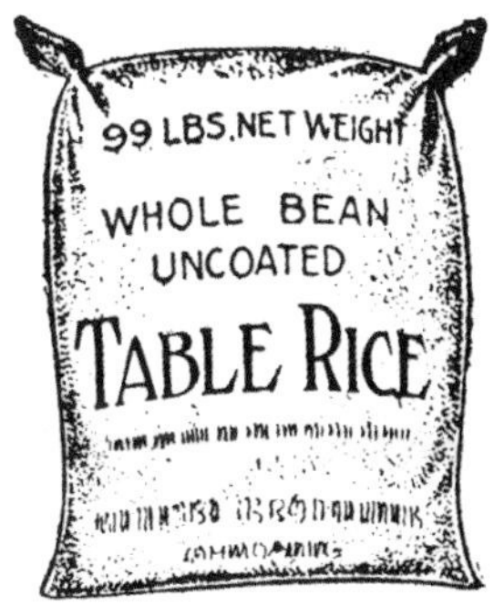

THE SECRET TO SUCCESSFUL HAGGLING IN MOROCCO

No one does haggling quite like the Moroccans, so the next time you find yourself in a *souk*, be aware of the hidden ground rules or you could find yourself paying way too much for a new carpet or exotic bird. Firstly, patience is crucial. Correct bartering etiquette requires time, which is something most Moroccan merchants have in spades. It is also considered respectful to think carefully when parting with something as important as money.

Once you show even the slightest iota of interest in a trader's wares, the game begins. Ask the price of something, and in a merchant's eyes you have already bought it. Sellers will start at double, triple, even ten times the amount they'd expect you to pay. Your first response should be a method-actor-worthy look of horror followed by a bid somewhere below half the asking price. Mentally decide on the top price you'll pay and stick with it. Once you reach it, keep repeating it over and over—the merchant will eventually get the point. And once you have both decided on a price, it is extremely rude to back out.

When dealing with antiques, ask the price first before asking about its provenance. That way, you will sound like a seasoned buyer. You can also use articles you have brought from home—pens, T-shirts, and so forth—to form part of the deal, especially if the seller has expressed an interest.

Another tip worth knowing is that Moroccans have their own pecking order of perceived wealth. The Japanese are charged the highest prices, then the Americans, and then the Europeans. So if you are after a genuine bargain, pretend you're from an obscure country with questionable economic stability. And don't feel too bad about embroidering the truth: Moroccan merchants are world-class salesmen and would never part with anything without turning a profit. ❀

THE SECRET OF CHARLES II

King Charles II was restored to the throne of England in 1660, 11 years after the execution of his father and the abolition of the monarchy. It is extraordinary that in the fevered religious atmosphere of 17th-century England he would sign a secret treaty that would risk his own neck, but he did precisely that. In 1670, Charles's sister and Louis XIV's sister-in-law Henriette-Anne signed the treaty of Dover with Charles, in which England and Louis XIV's France committed themselves to a joint attack on the Dutch Republic. In addition, a secret clause pledged Charles to declare himself a Catholic in the future, with France offering military support to quell the expected unrest. Historians dispute the extent of Charles's Catholic sympathies; he was received into the Church on his deathbed, but whether he intended to reconvert England is doubtful. The secret treaty of Dover was a spectacular gamble, therefore. His hands were observed to shake in 1674 when he denied to Parliament that any secret agreement had been made with Louis XIV. In 1987, a draft of the treaty was auctioned at Sotheby's in London for nearly £330,000.

THE SECRET FLIGHT TO CUBA

In spite of the official boycott, there is one commercial flight a day between Miami International and Havana, Cuba. However, there's no point in looking for details about the flight and certainly no way that you could book yourself onto it. The daily USA to Cuba flight does not appear on any information boards or publicly available schedules, and the only Americans permitted to fly on it are members of the press and media services.

If you do manage to wangle a trip on the flight—maybe you could get a writing assignment for your local newspaper?—do not expect to be able to prove to friends that you'd actually made the trip. On arrival in the socialist republic, instead of having their passports stamped with incriminating evidence of having been in the land of hand-rolled cigars, an entry visa is stamped on a square of paper and attached to the visiting journalist's passport with a paper clip. So there is no indelible record of the traveler having visited the island. And any cigars brought back are likely to be confiscated, of course.

All of which is historically bizarre, since the first international commercial passenger flight to depart America, in 1920, was to Cuba from South Florida.

THE SECRET LOCATION OF THE WOODSTOCK FESTIVAL

Woodstock remains the best-known rock festival of all time. It wasn't the first (Monterey, in 1967, beat it by two years), and it wasn't the biggest (Watkins Glen, in 1973, drew 600,000 to see The Band, the Allman Brothers, and Grateful Dead). But Woodstock was, well . . . *Woodstock*. And its reputation was such that it spawned not only an anthem (Joni Mitchell's "Woodstock"), a triple album, a double album, and a souvenir box-set, but also a three-hour documentary and two sequel events in 1994 and 1999.

But what's really weird is: Woodstock wasn't actually held at Woodstock.

When the organizers were looking for big names to headline the three-day event in August 1969, they found the big bands of the era just weren't available: The Beatles were in the process of splitting up and the Rolling Stones were preparing for their first American tour in three years (which would culminate in the tragedy of Altamont). That just left Bob Dylan, who hadn't made a preannounced concert appearance in three years. The legendary singer-songwriter's absence, however, had lent him an even more mythic status, so overtures were made. But no word came back from the Dylan camp. As the deadline loomed, names like Jimi Hendrix, Joan Baez, and The Who had all agreed to appear, but still Dylan wouldn't commit.

The festival site was at Bethel, in upstate New York, a good 40 miles away from Woodstock. But Woodstock was where Bob Dylan lived. It was to this small artistic community that Dylan had relocated following his 1966 bike crash; this was where he recorded the *Basement Tapes*; where he took up painting and trampolining. And, the organizers reasoned, by calling the festival "Woodstock" they might just tempt Dylan out of hiding.

So Woodstock it became. But that still didn't do it for Dylan. Two weeks after the actual event ("three days of peace, music, and love"), Bob Dylan did appear at a festival—but true to form, this one was three thousand miles away from home . . . on the Isle of Wight! And just why had the spokesman of his generation chosen a tiny island off the south coast of England to appear? "I wanted to see the home of Alfred Lord Tennyson."

THE SECRET OF THE EMPTY GRAVEYARD OF BRITISH INDIA

In a decaying park on the outskirts of Delhi in India stand about 40 empty plinths. They were originally put in place after independence from British rule and were supposed to hold statues from around India commemorating the British Raj.

The plinths stand in Coronation Durbar Park, which was originally created to mark the site of the apogee of the Raj, and was where King George V's coronation extravaganza was held in 1911. Although Queen Victoria had been declared Empress of India in 1877—and to mark the occasion the Indian tradition of holding extravagant court gatherings, or durbars, was revived—she did not attend her own durbar, and neither did her son, Edward VII, when a second one was held in his honor on his succession in 1901. Thus, when George V became the first reigning British monarch to visit India, his coronation durbar was an extravagant spectacle. The king and Queen Mary sat on golden thrones under a golden canopy, observing military displays and awarding decorations to bejewelled maharajahs. A light railway had been built to transport over 100,000 spectators to the event. Delhi, the king emperor declared, would henceforth be the capital of British India, replacing Calcutta. So, Coronation Durbar Park was created to mark the site of this high watermark of British rule in India.

After independence, it was resolved that this park would be used as a "graveyard" for the statues and symbols of the Raj—but this never happened and, today, the empty plinths give Coronation Durbar Park an air of desolation. The plain around is largely deserted, prone to flooding, and visited by only a few curious tourists.

SECRET EXPLOSIONS #1

It was the French who invented hand grenades. They first appeared in the 16th century. They were hollow orbs filled with shot and gunpowder and had a slow burning fuse that was lit before it was thrown. They were so named after the pomegranate, because as they exploded they resembled the multi-sectioned fruit coming apart.

※ ※ ※

No lawyer would like to admit it, but one of their own was responsible for creating the first weapon of mass destruction. The machine gun was patented by London barrister James Puckle, who registered the invention in 1718.

※ ※ ※

Anyone who has ever tried to watch the Brits play cricket will know how dull the game is. Supporters of cricket like it that way, they claim. A cricket fan will enjoy the opportunity afforded them by a game to drink warm beer in the sunshine and even snooze through a few "balls." However, what they don't know is that the first grenades developed in Britain were called Mills Bombs and were shaped and weighted exactly like a cricket ball. The British military figured, correctly, that most soldiers would be able to throw one 100 feet or more.

THE SECRET GRAVE AT KING'S CROSS STATION

King's Cross Station in London may now be best known as the hidden departure point for the Hogwarts Express, the train Harry Potter takes to school from Platform 9 and three-quarters. But according to legend, it is also the secret burial site of the ancient British warrior Queen Boudicca, who is buried nearby under Platform 10. In A.D. 60, after the death of her husband Prasutagus, king of the Iceni, and the brutalization of her family, she led a savage rebellion against Roman rule. After burning Colchester and St Albans, she marched on London, but her forces were finally defeated at the site of King's Cross station. The area used to be known as Battle Bridge, and Roman military equipment has been uncovered during construction work. Once defeat was inevitable, Boudicca and her daughters are said to have taken poison rather than be tortured and publicly humiliated by her Roman conquerors, and they were buried on the battlefield.

SECRET PARISIAN CINEMA FOUND

In September of 2004, police found a cinema-cum-restaurant in a cavern under the French capital's 16th *arrondissement*. When asked who built it and why, the authorities shook their head and shrugged in a Gallic kind of a way.

"We have no idea whatsoever," said a police spokesman. "There were two swastikas painted on the ceiling, but also celtic crosses and several stars of David, so we don't think it's extremists. Some sect or secret society, maybe." With that uniquely French air of insouciance the spokesman shrugged and finished with the line, "There are any number of possibilities."

There are 170 miles of tunnels, caves, galleries, and catacombs underneath Paris. The police stumbled on the cinema while on a training exercise across the Seine from the Eiffel Tower, under the Palais de Chaillot. Entering through a drain next to the Trocadero, they were confronted by a tarpaulin marked "Building Site, No Access," behind which was a desk and CCTV set to record anyone who entered (and triggered a tape of dogs barking).

Further down, the tunnel opened out into a vast cave—like an underground amphitheater—around 54 ft. underground. Here they found projection equipment, a screen, and tapes of a wide variety of films including 1950s film noir classics and more recent thrillers. There was nothing subversive, illegal, or offensive about their content.

An adjacent smaller cave contained a restaurant and bar. "There were bottles of whisky and other spirits . . . tables and chairs, a pressure-cooker for making couscous," the spokesman went on, barely concealing his admiration for the organization. "The whole thing ran off a professionally installed electricity system and there were at least three phone lines."

But when they returned with experts from the French electricity board three days later, the phone and electricity lines had been cut. "Do not," read a note left lying in the middle of the cavern floor, "try to find us."

Within days a group called the Perforating Mexicans claimed on French radio that the underground cinema was its work. Patrick Alk, author of a book on the urban underground exploration movement said the discovery was "a shame but not the end of the world." There were, he said, "a dozen more where that one came from." ⧗

SYSTEMS OF FOREIGN ELECTRONIC SURVEILLANCE IN THE U.S.

A professional in the field of technical surveillance countermeasure (TSCM) revealed the following about the U.S. government's tolerance of diplomatic electronic spying in the U.S., including the United Nations (notwithstanding international treaty and U.S. law prohibiting such spying), in 2003:

1. Britain, Canada, and Australia have greater latitude than other countries for electronic spying in the U.S.
2. Foreign governments can electronically spy on one another in the U.S. but not on U.S. citizens.
3. Electronic spying can be done only from diplomatically exempt locations, i.e., office, home, or vehicle.
4. Electronic spying can be done only by government officials, not private contractors hired for the purpose.
5. Private contractors are not likely to have as sophisticated equipment as governments and will almost certainly be detected by governmental targets and/or USG TSCM units.
6. Governments locate their premises to have line-of-sight of targets and to be nearby.
7. Orientation of visible antennae on government premises can indicate targets.

BRUCE SPRINGSTEEN'S SECRET APPEARANCES

The success of Bruce Springsteen's 1984 album *Born in the U.S.A.* cemented his position as the pre-eminent American rock & roller of the time. But immediately prior to its release, Springsteen liked to stick close to his New Jersey roots. While "Boss mania" was at its height, after being called the "Future of Rock & Roll" by a music magazine or six, Springsteen could still be found jamming with local bands in Asbury Park bars. Bleary-eyed drinkers could hardly believe their eyes when Bruce Springsteen bounded up on stage to join Bystander, Cats on a Smooth Surface, or John Eddie & the Front Runners to chug through some old-fashioned barroom boogie numbers. But the best-kept secret of Springsteen's entire career concerns his appearance at Asbury Park's Stone Pony on 8 January 1984, when the Boss came a firm second at the venue's weekly Sunday night joke-telling contest. His Italian joke didn't snare the top prize of $25, and Bruce Springsteen retired hurt, only to return later that night with his guitar to blast out Chuck Berry's "Carol" and Little Richard's "Lucille." Nobody was laughing then, either.

THE SECRET OF HAPPINESS

"THE SECRET OF HAPPINESS IS THIS: LET YOUR INTERESTS BE AS WIDE AS POSSIBLE, AND LET YOUR REACTIONS TO THE THINGS AND PERSONS THAT INTEREST YOU BE AS FAR AS POSSIBLE FRIENDLY RATHER THAN HOSTILE."
Bertrand Russell (*20th-century British philosopher*)

"THE SECRET OF HAPPINESS IS SOMETHING TO DO."
John Burroughs (*19th-century American author*)

THE SECRET OF A GOOD CUP OF COFFEE

Vietnam is the second biggest coffee producer in the world, after Brazil. This is in spite of the climate being unsuitable and the industry over-reliant on chemical fertilizers as they rotate crops too quickly, and, as a result, Vietnamese coffee being inferior. It is also cheaper, and therefore used to make instant coffee or to bulk up blends of better quality beans.

When coffee is brewed and dried to become instant granules, the process will destroy much of the natural aroma. It is therefore reintroduced to what reaches the consumer in the form of aromatic oils that react with the air once the jar's seal is broken.

Increased mechanization in coffee harvesting may be contributing to cancer. When coffee "cherries" (the fruit that is roasted to become the "bean") are picked by hand, the immature green fruit is left on the tree. Mechanized picking removes whole clusters of cherries and cannot differentiate between ripe and underripe. As there is no or very little hand sorting or checking, these green cherries get into the roasting system and are roasted into black beans which not only impair the grounds' flavor but are susceptible to a cancer-causing fungus.

THE SECRET OF ADAM'S CODE

When a child is reported missing in some large stores in the U.S., a security protocol, or series of steps, named "Code Adam" is adopted.

First a detailed description of the child is obtained from the parent or guardian, including his or her name, age, eye color, weight, height, shoe size, and a description of their clothing. Then the employee goes to the nearest in-store phone and pages "Code Adam" followed by the description. The greeter then begins monitoring the front door, and managers cover all other doors. The parking area is also checked. If the child is not found within ten minutes, the local authorities are contacted. If the child is found, an employee cancels Code Adam over the intercom.

So far, so procedural. What is more bizarre—and, some might say, distasteful—is that the code is named after Adam Walsh, a six-year-old boy who was abducted from the Sears store in Hollywood, Florida in 1981. His body was found 16 days after his disappearance and identified using dental records. At the time of Adam's abduction (for which there has been no arrest or conviction) no set procedure to deal with missing children in malls was in operation.

Urban legend, and probably the person who named the protocol on the other hand, confuses Adam's story with apocryphal—and always sensational—accounts of abductions often circulated via email. These tend to involve the drugging of a child and the dying of their hair or shaving of its head or application of a wig. All the stories are garbage and designed to feed people's worst fears. ⌛

THE SECRET OF BARGAIN HUNTING (CLOTHES)

Find a flaw. Point out the fault to the staff—you should get a discount of around 10 percent, depending on the damage. This is even more likely if you're a popular size (they'll have sold out of alternatives) or an odd size (they'll only have one sample in stock).

Only shop on a Thursday. That's when the majority of stores get their new stock delivered. Get there early and bag the best bargains.

Become skinny. A size six is a sample size designed to fit models. Most designers sell clothes worn on the catwalk or in showrooms at vastly discounted prices. Look for ads for sample sales in most city newspapers.

Only shop during the sales. And only on the first or last day. Best buys will have vanished after day one, but by the end the remainder will have been slashed to bargain-basement prices. Save time by visiting the store before the sale to decide what you want. ❀

SECRETS OF MARDI GRAS

The tradition of masked Mardi Gras parties in New Orleans dates back to the balls held during the period of French rule. The modern Mardi Gras celebrations have their origin in the founding in 1857 of the Mystick Krewe of Comus, a secret parading carnival group. Others followed, such as the Krewe of Rex in 1872, formed to entertain Russian royalty. More recently unorthodox krewes have emerged, such as the Mystic Krewe of Barkus, whose membership is restricted to dogs.

Even nowadays, it can be hard to join a krewe: you have to be sponsored by members, approved by a secret membership group, then put to an executive committee that votes on your admission. You never find out who the committee members are. Some clubs are more secretive than others, and since the introduction of anti-discrimination regulations in 1992, the more traditional and secretive krewes have ceased parading, preferring to hold private balls instead.

LITTLE KNOWN CULINARY CURIOS #2

The most reliable way to make a lumpy sauce is to attempt to mix flour and hot liquid together directly—the flour will start cooking immediately. Mix the flour with fat—not oil—first and cook the two together to form a "roux." Once the grains of the flour have started to open up the liquid will combine smoothly.

The secret to re-baking a cold baked potato is to dip it in water and give it 15 minutes in a very hot oven.

Cakes collapse if you open the oven door because heat expands air bubbles in the cake and makes it rise. A sudden rush of cold air reverses the process.

If you are steaming vegetables or fish, salt added to the water you are boiling will raise the temperature and cook your food quicker.

THE SECRET OF BARGAIN HUNTING (TRAVEL)

Plan carefully. Many business hotels offer reduced prices at weekends; similarly, many tourist hotels and packages are cheaper out of season.

Become an air courier. This is someone who carries documents for a courier company on international flights. They get discounted flights so this is a great way to see the world at a bargain. Approach individual courier companies for more details.

Shop around. Despite the deceptive name, no-frills airlines do not always offer the cheapest deals. With a little time and use of the internet you can root out the real bargains.

Become a vulture tourist. Travel to countries with unstable economies or former war-torn nations that have recently been removed from the official, state-issued no-go list. Yes it's ruthless, but this way you are guaranteed the best bargains—plus you will be helping their economy.

THE SECRET FIRST SCREENING OF STAR WARS

The film that we now know as the 10th most successful of all time had a very, *very* bad beginning. Once upon a very long time ago, at a private screening, George Lucas previewed his follow-up to *American Graffiti* to fellow directors Steven Spielberg, Francis Ford Coppola, Martin Scorsese, and Brian de Palma.

The film he unveiled was a rough cut of *Star Wars*. There wasn't any music, whole chunks of the plot were missing, and the galactic battle scenes hadn't been completed, so Lucas used stock footage of WWII dogfights to fill in. But the omens were not good—de Palma took Lucas to one side to commiserate. Indeed, no one, save Spielberg, thought that there was really any future in Lucas's futuristic adventure. Even the actors joined in: on being shown a rough draft of the script, Harrison Ford told the writer/director, "George, you can *type* this shit, but you sure can't say it!"

But Lucas was soon vindicated. On its release in 1977, *Star Wars* was an immediate hit and it went on to become the most successful film of all time, a title it held until it was overtaken five years later by *ET*, directed by none other than Steven Spielberg.

SHRIMP SURVIVAL

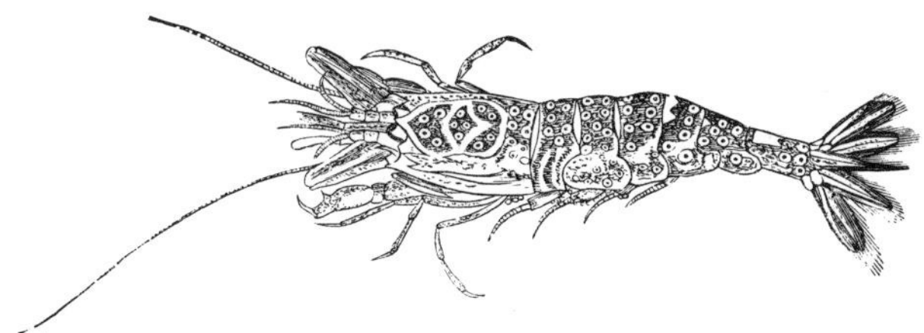

Most shrimps get a raw deal out of life. Small and light, they are buffeted by underwater currents and lack any of the heavy-duty survival weaponry wielded by their crustacean cousins, the crab and lobster. But one shrimp has evolved a most ingenious form of camouflage. It looks just like a piece of underwater grass and, as if that were not enough, it also comes in a variety of different colors (green, brown, and black). When a group of these shrimps are together they look just like pieces of grass in varying states of decay.

FAMOUS EUROPEAN FREEMASONS

ALEXANDER POPE
British poet, satirist, and critic, author of *The Rape of The Lock*, 1712

WILLIAM HOGARTH
British engraver and artist, painted *A Rake's Progress* in 1735

EDWARD GIBBON
British historian, author of *The History of the Decline and Fall of the Roman Empire*, 1776

WOLFGANG AMADEUS MOZART
Austrian composer, became a Freemason in Vienna in 1781

ROBBIE BURNS
Scottish poet, author of "Auld Lang Syne" and "Address to A Haggis," 1786

EDMUND BURKE
British political philosopher, author of *Reflections on the Revolution in France*, 1790

DR. EDWARD JENNER
British scientist and inventor of vaccination, 1796

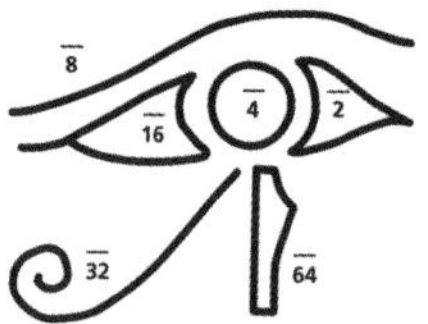

JOHANN WOLFGANG VON GOETHE
German playwright, author of *Faust*, 1808

SIR WALTER SCOTT
Scottish writer and poet, author of *Lady of the Lake*, 1810

DUKE OF WELLINGTON
British military commander at Waterloo where he defeated Napoleon of France, 1815; credited with inventing the Wellington boot

SIR WILLIAM GILBERT
British opera composer, co-author of various operettas such as *Patience*, 1881 and *The Mikado*, 1885

SIR ARTHUR SULLIVAN
British opera composer, co-author of various operettas such as *Patience*, 1881 and *The Mikado*, 1885

ANTHONY TROLLOPE
British writer (*The Way We Live Now*, 1875); inventor of the red post box (1864)

DR. T. J. BARNARDO
Irish medical missionary, opened his first home for destitute boys in London, 1870

SIR ARTHUR CONAN DOYLE
British writer, author of the Sherlock Holmes novels 1887–1927

CECIL RHODES
British politician and prospector; the creator of the British South Africa Company; prime minister of Cape Colony 1890; bequeathed the Rhodes Scholarship at Oxford for Teutonic races only, 1902

RUDYARD KIPLING
British writer and poet, author of *The Jungle Book*, 1894 and *Kim*, 1901

SIR HENRY IRVING
British stage actor and troupe leader, the first actor to be knighted, 1895

CAPT. ROBERT FALCON SCOTT
British explorer, leader of the Antarctic expedition 1901–1904 and again in 1907

HAROLD ABRAHAMS
British athlete, the second non-American to win the 100-meter gold medal at the Paris Olympics, 1924

SIR ALEXANDER FLEMING
Scottish discoverer of penicillin, 1928

KING EDWARD VIII
British monarch, ascended to the throne January 1936, abdicated December 1936 for the love of US divorcée Wallis Simpson

KING GEORGE VI
British monarch ascended to the throne December 1936, died February 1952; the father of Queen Elizabeth II

SIR LEN HUTTON
British cricketer, held the record for highest Test score for 20 years, 1938-1958

SIR WINSTON CHURCHILL
British prime minister between 1940 and 1945 and again between 1951 and 1955; made an honorary U.S. citizen in 1963 by President John F. Kennedy

TOMMY TRINDER
British comedian, star of British comedy movies in the 1940s, first master of ceremonies for TV show *Sunday Night At The Palladium*, 1955

SIR WILLIAM "BILLY" BUTLIN
British, opened the first holiday camp in England, 1963

JOCK STEIN
Scottish soccer manager of Celtic 1965–1978, manager of Scotland national team from 1978 until his death from a heart attack in 1985

PETER SELLERS
British comic actor, star of the *Pink Panther* movies; Oscar nominated as best actor for *Being There*, 1981

THE SECRETS OF BLACK MAGIC

Compiled in the medieval and early modern periods, "grimoires" were handbooks of magical knowledge—practical guides to astrology, demonology, necromancy, and similar dark arts. A venerable tradition was claimed on behalf of the grimoire, and King Solomon was the purported author of works known as the *Lesser Key* and the *Greater Key*. Grimoires set out in detail the form and liturgy of magical and satanic rituals. For example, a Black Sabbath should ideally be conducted in a clearing in the woods. Behind the black altar a figure represents the Devil, either a goat or a cat, flanked by symbolic "brides." The company assemble in a semicircle in front of the altar. The priest, in a cloak decorated with a pentagram, holds a black turnip aloft and recites a long prayer to the Devil: "Oh Satan, you who are the shadow of God and of ourselves, I speak these words of agony for your glory . . ." The initiates are brought naked and blindfolded in front of the company, where they affirm their belief in black magic in a form of unholy catechism: "I deny God, and all religion . . . I will always swear by the name of the Devil . . ." They then perform the "osculum obscoenum," kissing the Devil figure's backside. Then it is the time for feasting, dancing, copulation, and possibly drug-taking. By daybreak the area is cleared of any traces of the night's satanic activities.

To perform black magic, the wizard should wear black robes and a lead cap inscribed with the signs of the Moon, Venus, and Saturn. Depending on the nature of the ceremony, the colors of the robe could be altered: red for vengeance, sky blue for sexual magic, and white for benign magic. A circle would be laid out with strips of goatskin, and a triangle traced out inside, starting from the eastern point. The warlock would stand in the triangle in front of a brazier, flanked by candles. Having offered up a prayer to the Devil, he could proceed with the ritual.

In order to fly, witches and warlocks would smear their bodies with magical unguent. One recipe included aconite boiled with polar leaves and parsley, while another one combines water hemlock, sweet flag, cinquefoil, bat's blood, and oil. Aconite and water hemlock are both poisons and could cause dizziness or delirium if inhaled or rubbed into the skin. Mandrake was another poisonous plant extensively used in magic and witchcraft. It was believed to be half-plant, half-human, and was thought to scream when pulled from the earth.

ABANDONED NEW YORK SUBWAY STATIONS #3

HOYT-SCHERMERHORN STREETS

LOCATION: AT HOYT, SCHERMERHORN, AND BOND STREETS

OPENED IN APRIL 1936, CLOSED JUNE 1946. RE-OPENED SEPTEMBER 1959, CLOSED MARCH 1981.

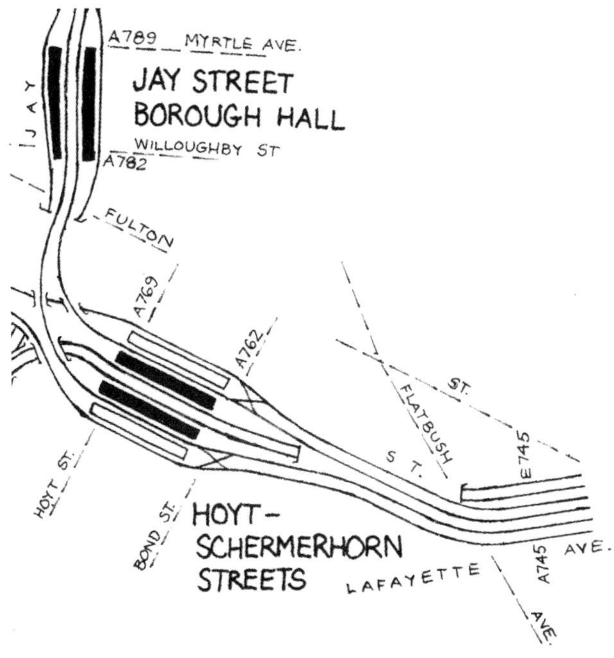

Like Court Street, this station was part of an independent subway system built by the Board of Transportation. Originally closed in 1946 along with Court Street, Hoyt-Schermerhorn Sts. was used again from 1959 to 1981 for Aqueduct Racetrack special trains, since it was the only stop between 42 St. at 8 Ave. and the track. It is now sometimes used as a movie set as was formerly done at Court St.

ELVIS'S SECRET RECORDING

The world knows and loves Elvis's hits—from "That's All Right (Mama)" to "Way Down," the King sold millions of records. But there's one recording that has never been mentioned in anyone's list of their favorite Elvis recordings. "You can get 'em piping hot, after 4pm; you can get 'em piping hot. Southern Maid Doughnuts hit the spot . . ." were the lyrics to perhaps not the most exciting advertising jingle ever, but it was the only one that Elvis Presley ever sang.

On 6 November 1954, the 19-year-old was fourth on the bill at the Louisiana Hayride and like a lot of other performers on the show, Elvis sang the praises of the show's sponsors, Southern Maid Doughnuts. He may not have made much money, but the teenager sure got a lot of complimentary doughnuts.

THE SECRET VATICAN ARCHIVES

These private records of the pope extend over 50 miles of shelves and consist of around 10 million pages of documents. The secret archives were first opened to scholars in 1881. But like any government, there is a significant time lag and any document deemed to be particularly harmful may be kept hidden. Currently, the archives can be accessed up to the period of Benedict XV (1914-1922), though in 2006 documents relating to the pontificate of Pius XI (1922-1939) will open to scrutiny. This period saw the coming to power of the European dictators and the first implementation of anti-Jewish racial laws in Germany and Italy. However, it is the secret archive of his successor, Pius XII, which is most eagerly anticipated by scholars. Pius's reputation has been the subject of furious debates, principally over the nature of the Vatican's relationship with the Nazi regime and the pope's attitude toward the Jews of Europe.

THE SECRET OF SAN DIEGO'S WGASA LINE

In the San Diego Wild Animal Park is a monorail which runs around a huge enclosure, allowing visitors to observe the animals within. It is known as the Wgasa line. Why Wgasa? In 1972 busy staff at the new park were struggling to think of a name for the monorail when the chief designer suggested a then well-known acronym which reflected both their struggle and their attitude toward it. The name stuck and spread so quickly that it was kept. The acronym stood for "Who Gives a Shit Anyway?"

AN ANCIENT SECRET WEAPON

When the port of Syracuse (in modern-day Sicily) was threatened with attack by the Romans in 213 B.C., the Greek mathematician Archimedes was employed to defend his city. His ingenuity and scientific know-how led him to design a devastating device that successfully repelled the Roman fleet. Although no drawings survive of his "secret weapon," the writer Plutarch gave a description of its catastrophic deployment against the Romans. Archimedes's "claw" was a boom-like weapon that swung out from over the city walls, ensnaring enemy ships, lifting them up into air, shaking them so the sailors were thrown off, and smashing them on the water or rocks.

SECRET WATCHDOGS

In ancient Rome, the top of the Capitoline Hill was the site of temples devoted to Jupiter, Minerva, and Juno. The temple of Juno, in an area now occupied by the Chiesa di Santa Maria in Aracoeli, was where the sacred Capitoline geese were kept. According to legend, it was geese—not guard dogs—that raised the alarm in 390 B.C. when the city was under attack by the Gauls. In the annual Roman commemoration of the event, geese were carried in honor on gold and purple cushions, while dogs, which had failed to bark when intruders were attacking, were crucified.

THE SECRET OF EATING YOUR WAY TO A BETTER SEX LIFE

We all know about the potent power of oysters—Casanova, for instance, is said to have eaten 50 of them raw during his morning bath using a gorgeous woman's breast as his plate—but it's not only shellfish that can boost your libido.

Chocolate is good for many things. Casanova was a fan of it, of course—he religiously ate a chunk every time he had sex. Likewise the Aztecs consumed ground cocoa beans before partaking in any acts of romantic passion. Chocolate works to heighten sexual activity because it contains the chemical theobromine, which is a proven aid to arousal, while another chemical to be found in chocolate is phenylethylamine, which produces the same fuzzy feeling that humans experience when they're in love. And as if that wasn't enough, chocolate also stimulates the secretion of endorphins, otherwise known as the happiness hormone.

Truffles, those musty-smelling rare fungi, contain chemicals similar to the sex hormones found in the male pig, which is why farmers only send female pigs out to snuffle for them. Curiously, these chemicals are also very similar to the sex hormones found in men, hence their aphrodisiac quality. Although many women actually find the scent a turn-off, studies show that the male nose is more receptive to truffle scent than the female.

Vanilla is another scent that sends men wild. If you want to attract male attention, scientific research proves this is the single smell they find most seductive.

Nutmeg was considered by the Arabs, Greeks, and Romans as an essential aid to lovemaking. The same reverence for the spice is held in India where Hindus regularly consume a mixture of nutmeg, honey, and half a boiled egg to prolong their performance.

Onions don't just make you cry and your breath smell. Again, both Arabs and Hindus consider the humble onion an aphrodisiac—in fact, so powerful were its qualities considered that monks were once banned from eating them. The French are big fans, of course: according to tradition, a newlywed Gallic couple are served onion soup the day after their wedding to restore their sexual powers.

Celery is beneficial to both sexes. For men, it can cure impotence and attract the opposite sex thanks to its stimulation of androsterone, a male hormone normally released through sweat. For women, because of the same hormone, consumption of celery increases her chances of having a boy.

Ginger, as long as it is fresh, is a godsend for men. The powerful root helps those suffering from erectile dysfunction—such is its power that it actually widens the blood vessels in the pelvic region—as well as those hoping to become a father since the spice increases the sperm count. In fact, this is the origin of gingerbread men. According to legend, single girls would bake the biscuits in the hope of attracting a husband.

Asparagus certainly looks sexy—and it is, to many people. In the 19th century, French grooms ate the vegetable before the big day to ensure they would be able to perform. Unlike most of the other foods listed here, however, there is no scientific proof that it actually works—with asparagus, it's all down to the imagination.

Beef: An organic bloody steak is brilliant for men. It's high in tyrosine, an amino acid that creates a feeling of euphoria, as well as the chemicals dopamine and norepinephrine, both of which work wonders on improving concentration. The heady combination of all three natural gems boosts and strengthens the male libido. ❀

THE SECRET OF SUCCESSFUL SLOGAN WRITING

Slogan writing is a knack like any other. Here are some tips from the experts:

1. INCLUDE A PUN IF YOU CAN

Focus on the task at hand and think of words associated with the product.

2. BE FUNNY

Check with friends that you are right but don't be too sophisticated—you are more likely to be rewarded for being relevant than being a literary genius.

3. IF IN DOUBT

Make it rhyme.

4. IF STILL IN DOUBT

Use alliteration.

5. WORK OUT A QUIRKY FACT ABOUT THE PRODUCT

There are X bubbles in the average bottle of X beer.

6. IF IT'S NOT STIPULATED, KEEP IT BRIEF

Judges may have hundreds, even thousands of entries to wade through. ⌛

THE SECRET TO STACKING BREAD

Each loaf of bread sold in a supermarket has a colored twist tie around it that serves a duel purpose. Not only does it keep the bread in the bag but it tells the shelf stacker how fresh it is. Each day of the week is assigned a color, presumably allowing the stacker to ensure that the oldest loaves are placed in the most prominent position. As a customer, one might not know the store or company's code without asking, but if there are loaves of bread with three different colors of twist tie on a shelf they deserve closer inspection of the "Best Before Date" since one of them is to be avoided. Even if there are two colors, armed with this information, it is possible to identify the freshest.

THE SECRET HISTORY OF THE TOWER OF LONDON

The Tower of London has a fearsome reputation as the scene of bloody persecution, imprisonment, and violent death. It's true that in the Tudor years many royal and political opponents from Anne Boleyn to Lady Jane Grey, and Thomas More to Thomas Cromwell were executed there by royal decree. What's less known is that for a period of over 150 years—since the beheading of the Scottish Jacobite Simon 11th Lord Lovat on 9 April 1747—no executions took place in the Tower. Until, that is, the First World War, when 11 Germans convicted of espionage were shot there. The last execution took place during the Second World War in 1941, when Josef Jakobs, a German who had been convicted of spying, was strapped to a chair and shot by firing squad. Ironically, the last person to die in the Tower was visitor Dorothy Household in 1974. She was killed when a bomb, thought to be planted by the IRA, went off in the White Tower.

A CLOCKWORK ORANGE SECRET

Stanley Kubrick's 1971 film *A Clockwork Orange* was recently voted the most rock & roll movie ever made. But not long after its release, Kubrick himself withdrew the film after a number of "copycat killings," although its unavailability only added luster to the legend. Heaven 17, Moloko, and Campag Velocet were just three of the rock bands who took their names from the film. So did Echo & The Bunnymen's label, Korova. As Ziggy Stardust, David Bowie regularly made his stage entrance to Walter (later Wendy) Carlos's synthesizer theme to *A Clockwork Orange*. Kubrick's masterpiece was also the only film that the Rolling Stones almost made—imagine Mick Jagger as Alex in a film directed by David Bailey, anyone? Later, not to be outdone, U2's Bono and the Edge wrote the score for the Royal Shakespeare Company's 1990 production of *A Clockwork Orange*.

But it was the soundtrack of the film that hid *A Clockwork Orange*'s greatest secret. Amidst the futuristic synthesizer of Carlos, and the rousing music of Rossini, Beethoven, and Elgar, how did the mightily obscure Sunforest land not just one, but *two* tracks ("Overture to the Sun" and "I Want to Marry a Lighthouse Keeper") on the *Clockwork Orange* soundtrack album?

All that's really known about the band is that Sunforest was a trio of American girls who recorded only one album, *The Sound of Sunforest*, which was released on the Deram label in 1970. It was that album that somehow caught Kubrick's attention. And the rest is soundtrack history . . .

THE SECRET OF MY SUCCESS

"EIGHTY PERCENT OF SUCCESS IS SHOWING UP."
Woody Allen (*20th-century American comedian*)

"I DON'T KNOW THE KEY TO SUCCESS, BUT THE KEY TO FAILURE IS TRYING TO PLEASE EVERYBODY."
Bill Cosby (*20th-century American comedian*)

THE SECRET HISTORY OF STRIPTEASE

The World's Columbian Exposition was held in Chicago in 1893 to celebrate the 400th anniversary of Christopher Columbus's first voyage to America. The Exposition was held on a site along Chicago's south lakefront, an area now encompassed by Jackson Park and the Midway Plaisance, and was mocked up with numerous foreign city streets to provide an exotic "world tour." One enterprising entrepreneur by the name of Sol Bloom successfully staged the first public performances of "exotic dancing"—or striptease—in the "civilized" world.

As Sol thumped a vaguely Eastern melody on an old upright piano (he'd devised the Hoochy Coochy earlier that day), a small woman of Middle-Eastern appearance shimmied barefoot onto a stage in the middle of the specially constructed Cairo Street set and began swaying and removing layers of diaphanous clothing. A small cardboard sign set on an easel at the side of the stage said, simply, "Little Egypt." As the dancer threw away her "veils," her ankle bells tinkled and the hearts of a thousand top-hatted businessmen pounded like steam engines. Sol's event was such a success that an industry grew up around "Little Egypt," including slot machines bearing her name and exotic dancers touring America by the end of the century, all claiming to be her. The business of striptease had been high-kick started. ⌛

SECRET CHRISTIAN CATACOMBS

The ancient Romans cremated their dead and forbade burials of bodies within the city limits. The early Christians dug out over 200 miles of tunnels outside the city of Rome and used recesses within the passageways as tombs, and as a place where they could practice their faith unmolested. The catacombs now provide the earliest example of Christian art in the remaining sculptures, sarcophagi, frescoes, and inscriptions. One recurring theme in this artwork is the Christian "fish"—still used today on U.S. cars and business cards to identify those who follow the Christian faith. The fish was an important ancient symbol of Christianity used in parables such as that of the loaves and fishes. But the Greek word for fish—"ICHTHYS"—was also used as a religious acrostic by the early Christians as a credo to express their faith and as a secret means to identify each other. The Greek letter "I" referred to Jesus, or "Iesus" as he was then known; the "CH" to Christos or Christ; the "TH" to Theou or God; the "Y" to Yios or son; and the "S" to Soter or savior. The meaning is "Jesus Christ God Son Savior."

DYLAN THOMAS'S SECRET LAST DRINK . . .

Everyone thinks Dylan Thomas's last drink was whisky imbibed at an English-style pub on Hudson Street in Greenwich Village, the White Horse Tavern. After a drinking session there on 3 November 1953, his reported last words were, "I've had 18 straight whiskies—I think that's the record." But the next day, while complaining of feeling ill, he went out with a friend and downed a couple of beers before returning to his hotel and calling a doctor. After various medical interventions he fell into a coma later that night, and died on 9 November at St. Vincent's Hospital.

WHY THE BRITISH DRINK SO MUCH

In the 18th century somebody who drank too much beer would be known as a "malt worm." Yet at the time, it wasn't uncommon for doctors to prescribe white ale (a pale ale fermented with a mixture of yeast, malt flour, and egg white) to nursing mothers to increase their milk, and even to give to babies as a cure for colic. And never mind a tot of rum, King Henry VIII's navy enjoyed an allowance of a gallon of beer per man per day, even when they were fighting a campaign. The British fought on alcohol, even if it meant a rise in price—the Boer War (1900) was largely paid for by a 24 percent hike in the tax on beer in the UK. King Henry VIII's military campaigns included mobile breweries at the frontline, so the troops could get a pint after a hard day's war.

A fashionable drink in Georgian times was a mug of "mild and stale," which was about three parts freshly brewed, sweeter ale, topped off with one part of more bitter mature ale to round out the flavor. The term "stale" meant "still," as mature beer would be clearer than a new brew—the word wasn't used as the opposite of "fresh" until the middle of the 19th century.

A "brewer's pound" is not a conventional unit of weight, but the number of pounds of sugar needed to be dissolved in water for it to attain a particular specific gravity.

What used to be called Milk Stout, made famous by the Mackeson brewery in pre-WWII Britain, was dark beer brewed not with milk but with milk-derived lactose sugar.

Gin houses came to prominence in the mid-18th century, threatening beer's popularity as the lower class's favored route to oblivion—industrial-strength gin was sold at a penny for five fluid ounces, as opposed to beer at thrupence a mug (around half a pint). So serious was the effect of gin on Britain's urban poor that three successive Acts of Parliament were passed between 1729 and 1743 to control the sale of gin, but it was only the last one, which hiked up duty to a point where it was priced out of the working-class market, that had any effect. It's at this point that gin's snob value took root as suddenly the proletariat couldn't afford it.

Britain's earliest known large-scale brewery was among excavated Roman ruins at Chorleywood, Herfordshire, and dates back to the first century A.D.

At the beginning of the 19th century London was the epicenter of the beer brewing universe: the world's biggest brewery (Truman's) was in the capital, innovations in style and type were taking place there, and more beer per head of the population was being made and consumed.

A 1907 Act of Parliament, pushed through by a Temperance Movement-driven Liberal government (surely a contradiction in terms?) prohibited women from working in pubs, as, apparently, the notion of an attractive barmaid was encouraging men to spend too much time drinking. There was a demonstration of over half a million people (mostly men) in Hyde Park as a protest and although the Bill was passed by Parliament, it didn't get through the House of Lords a year later.

The notion of "Closing Time," and the break in afternoon opening from 3:00 to 5:30, was introduced in Britain as part of the 1914 Defence of the Realm Act. The popularly quoted reason is that excess drinking was hampering the war effort, yet the act went through a mere three days after Germany and Austria-Hungary declared war in August of that year. Hardly time to get a round in, let alone affect munitions production. It was actually widely perceived to be one more aspect of the Liberal government's ongoing war with the drinks industry. During the next year, Lloyd George, who was then Chancellor, lost no opportunity to talk about Britain fighting three enemies "Germany, Austria, and drink . . . and the greatest of these three deadly foes is drink." He attempted to bring about complete prohibition in the UK, but Parliament wouldn't go so far as an outright ban. Bizarrely though, what did get through was a ban on buying an alcoholic drink for somebody other than yourself—"treating" as it was described in the Bill—as it was believed that the buying of rounds encouraged people to drink more than they would if left alone. It would be 74 years before pubs could open all day again with the Licensing Act of 1988, and over 80 years (August 1995) before they could open all day on Sunday.

THE SECRETS OF CASANOVA'S SUCCESS

Giovanni Giacomo Casanova is widely considered the greatest seducer who ever lived. But what, exactly, was the secret of the 18th-century lover's success? For a start it seems that his background helped. He was born into a family of actors and spent much of his working life as a secret agent, so he was involved in professions that require a mastery of manipulation and charm. He also grew up in a family full of women, so had years of insight into how the female psyche worked. Consequently, he was a renowned conversationalist, had excellent manners, and was highly knowledgeable about the arts.

His specific methods for seduction, however, were surprisingly simple. For Casanova to get results, all it took was usually a little time (although he wasn't averse to it taking longer) and effort. First, he studied his prey. He followed a lady's moods and worked out what was missing from her life, then strived to fill that gap by assuming a suitable persona.

He was a social chameleon and highly adaptable. In his own words, he would "Praise the beautiful for their intelligence and the intelligent for their beauty." Casanova would somehow manage to penetrate a woman's mind and always made sure that the seduction was all about her, not about him.

Another favorite trick of the serial seducer was to arrive at a first meeting wearing flamboyant clothes and covered in jewels. He would gauge her reaction: how much work would he have to do? Was she an impressionable young thing who could be bowled over by looks? Or was she a tougher, more skeptical, nut to crack?

Casanova would often tease his prey. With one Milanese countess he hoped to seduce, he produced a beautiful sable-trimmed red dress as he was unpacking at her house. When she asked whom the dress was for, he simply replied it was a gift for the Milanese woman to whom he was most attracted. And so the game began.

Casanova would gradually seduce his victims, drawing out the courtship for as long as possible—he often said he enjoyed the foreplay just as much as, if not more than, the eventual conquest. Unsurprisingly, his intentions were never long-term—he never wished to marry—but unlike a mere cad or a simple charmer, he would always end the affair perfectly, perhaps introducing his lover to a more suitable man. He would cry crocodile tears, give his reasons (which were always spun to sound as if they were beneficial for her), leave a generous gift, and then vanish.

Casanova's own stated secret of his astonishing success with women was put succinctly thus: "The easiest way to overcome a woman's virtue is to assume it is not there in the first place." ❀

THE SECRET READING LIST

FIVE BOOKS THAT HAVE TO BE READ IN SECRET IN SOME PARTS OF AMERICA:

THE JOY OF SEX, AND MORE JOY OF SEX BY ALEX COMFORT

In 1978, these books were banned by Lexington police in accordance with a new county law prohibiting the display of sexually orientated publications in places frequented by minors.

THE ADVENTURES OF HUCKLEBERRY FINN BY MARK TWAIN

The world "nigger" appears throughout this book. In 1984, it was removed from an eighth-grade reading list in Waukegan, Illinois, because an alderman found it offensive. In the fall of 2003, the Renton School District removed it from their approved reading list.

AS I LAY DYING BY WILLIAM FAULKNER

In 1986, the school board at Graves County, Kentucky—none of whom, it is alleged, had read the book—banned this from its high school English reading list. They banned it because it contained seven passages which referred to God or abortion, and included words such as "bastard," "goddam," and "son of a bitch."

SNOW FALLING ON CEDARS BY DAVID GUTERSON

In 2000, after a community debate it was decided by the South Kitsap County School District board that this award-winning book should be removed from the reading list, allegedly due to its sexual content, language, and promotion of intolerance.

THE HARRY POTTER SERIES BY J. K. ROWLING

In 2003, a Church group from Greenville, Michigan burned this series on the basis that it concerned itself with the dark arts. The group felt it should be made known that the books were about witchcraft. ⌛

FOOD STUFF THEY'D RATHER YOU DIDN'T KNOW #1

Modified Atmosphere Packaging (MAP) is the "air" that surrounds the leaves in sealed bags of pre-packed salad, and it will have an increased carbon dioxide content at the expense of oxygen. While this is what stops the salad leaves from wilting and discoloring for anything up to a month, it will greatly reduce the leaves' Vitamin C and E content.

Health authorities recommend washing pre-packed salad before eating it, even though it is sold as being already washed, because there is a very high probability of it being washed in a strong chlorine solution.

Ginko and ginseng may do wonders for concentration, but by stimulating blood flow to the brain they can also contribute to or trigger migraines and headaches. If you are a migraine sufferer it is wisest to stay away from such herbal supplements.

The incidents of fruit- or vegetable-related food poisoning have more than doubled in the last decade, with salmonella and E. coli being the front runners.

Blended cooking oils should be avoided, as they will contain palm or coconut oil, which are both relatively very high in saturated fats.

It is estimated that, on or in their food, the average adult consumes 10 liters of pesticide a year. Carefully wash any fruit or vegetable that is not going to be peeled.

Coffee beans lose most of their flavor during the decaffination process, and it has to be reintroduced artificially. 🖫

SECRETS OF AIR TRAVEL

There are numerous entertaining urban myths surrrounding the matter of air travel. This is probably because the business of flying is opaque at the best of times. Take the matter of getting an upgrade, for instance. Never mind wearing a suit or flashing a smile, "free" upgrades to business class or first class are based on one thing only: how much you paid for your ticket. If the flight can sell more economy class seats than it has available, passengers who have paid full fare (or nearest to it) will be bumped up to create extra seats at the back.

Why the price of airline tickets for the same journey can vary from day to day, or even from minute to minute, is because the airline's central computer is perpetually calculating how much that flight needs to earn to make the required profit, and will readjust the fares after each ticket is sold.

Overbooking is policy on every airline except those based in Japan. Taking reservations for more passengers than the aircraft will hold is to ensure the flight is still full after the usual number of "no shows" (on average two percent of every flight) have been accounted for. Japanese airlines claim they do not overbook because Japanese travelers wouldn't dream of missing a flight they had reserved a seat on.

THE SECRET LANGUAGE OF TATTOOS

Within the vast gulag and prison system of the former Soviet Union, tattoos played a highly symbolic role in the world of the Russian criminal class. They referred to their sets of tattoos as "decorated tailcoats" and used them to express their own personal history and attitudes, including criminal records, places of incarceration, or expressions of love and loss. Seemingly commonplace images would often communicate a complicated series of meanings: for example, a raised leopard with the word "MIR" (Russian for "peace") inscribed in it also works as an acronym meaning "shooting would reform me." The Russian word "BOG" (which means "God") is also an acronym for "I shall rob again." Russian criminal tattoos are both a statement of alienation from normal society, and a guide to where the person stood within the hierarchy of their bandit milieu.

ABANDONED NEW YORK SUBWAY STATIONS #4

18 STREET

LOCATION: AT 18 STREET AND PARK AVENUE

OPENED IN OCTOBER 1904, CLOSED IN NOVEMBER 1948.

Much like Worth Street, the station is just below street level and has no mezzanine. Unlike Worth Street, however, after a first platform extension in 1910, the post-WWII platform extensions that occurred across the city brought about the closure of 18 St. Since it had only been opened as a half mile stop between stations, the transit authority deemed it surplus to requirements. There are two short platforms and an unremarkable station. It was so ordinary when built that it was used for publicity photographs for the subway as an example of how all stations looked.

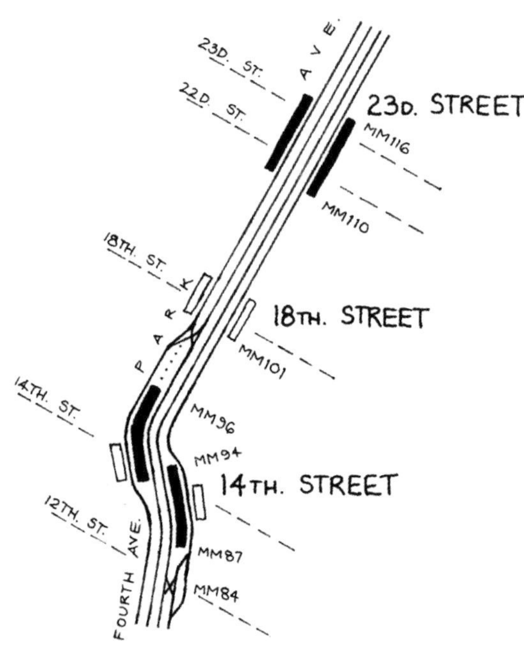

CIA MIND CONTROL EXPERIMENTS

By the early 1950s, the American intelligence community was in a heightened state of paranoia—and it had seemingly infected the whole of the country with the same paranoia. The Soviet Union had exploded atomic weapons, Red China was increasingly seen as a threat, and at home Senator Joseph McCarthy was leading a hunt for domestic communists which had taken in movie stars, writers, and other assorted media figures.

Amid this wave of paranoia-inducing activity, fears that the Russians had developed brainwashing chemicals emerged, having been inspired by the "confessions" of American prisoners captured during the Korean War. Desperate for any advantage, the CIA turned their resources and attention to creating their own mind control experiments. In 1953 a secret project, codenamed MK-ULTRA, was set up, overseen by the scientist Sidney Gottlieb. Experiments were conducted using LSD, whose hallucinogenic qualities had been first identified that year by Dr. Albert Hoffman. It was thought that the drug could have wide applications in the interrogation of prisoners and the disorientation of enemies.

To begin with, CIA officers tried the drug on themselves, but soon the experiments took a darker turn. LSD was administered to unwary subjects, with prisoners and mental patients acting as human guinea pigs. Even more bizarrely, the CIA set up a series of brothels, where the effects of the drug were observed on prostitutes' clients through two-way mirrors. Some members of the security service envisaged a role for LSD in large-scale warfare, using it to disable entire cities through the water supply (an idea that was used as a threat by hippies in the 1960s).

However, tragedy struck when CIA employee Dr. Frank Olson jumped to his death from an upper floor of a New York hotel. It was alleged that he had become suicidal after being slipped some LSD. Dr. Olson's family have questioned the circumstances of his death ever since and his son maintains that he was murdered to prevent him revealing the U.S. army's use of anthrax in the Korean War. Ironically, the wider availability of LSD would help fuel the 1960s' anti-war movement and the prevailing mood against militarism.

Secret experiments using LSD were not confined to the U.S. intelligence and military establishment, though. In the 1950s the Secret Intelligence Service MI6 had conducted its own secret tests of LSD on British servicemen. These had taken place at Porton Down, the chemical warfare establishment, but had been swiftly abandoned after it was feared that the drug might provoke suicidal tendencies.

THE SECRET RESTING PLACE OF THE CROSS

The Chiesa di Santa Croce in Gerusalemme church in Rome was founded in A.D. 320 by Helena, the mother of the Emperor Constantine the Great. She had traveled to Jerusalem and brought back a collection of Christian relics from the Holy Land. They are now kept in a reliquary dating from the Fascist era, and include fragments of the "true" Cross, thorns from Christ's crown, and the finger that a skeptical St. Thomas used to probe Christ's wounds.

THE SECRET TO UNLOCKING A WOMAN'S SEX DRIVE

There is a scientifically proven way to increase a woman's sex drive, although unfortunately it requires male stamina and the ability to follow through on the common promise to "phone the next day." Which is apparently impossible for most men. The key to unlocking a woman's sex drive is all down to oxytocin, a bonding chemical found in the brain. Oxytocin is known as the human attachment hormone, and its various functions include aiding milk production during lactation and uterine contractions during childbirth. But it's the fact that the hormone is also released by both sexes during orgasm that holds the key to the female sex drive. Women naturally have oxytocin in spades, and their levels shoot up even more during sexual intercourse. Oxytocin in turn stimulates testosterone production, the hormone responsible for the sex drive in both men and women, which is why the more a woman has sex, the more she will want it.

A man's oxytocin levels, on the other hand, can be up to ten times lower than the average woman's, even a woman who is celibate. In fact, the only time a man's levels reach a point anywhere near a woman's is when he ejaculates. But his oxytocin levels will quickly fall again post-sex. Which is why he won't phone the next day, even if he said he loved you and could never live without you. Sorry, but that was just his oxytocin speaking.

FRYING PAN SECRETS

In terms of non-stickability and even control of heat, cast iron is the best material for a frying pan, closely followed by heavyweight aluminum. Stainless steel is the worst.

Non-stick frying pans have a much shorter life than you might expect: when even slightly worn, overheating can cause the surface to release potential carcinogens, noxious gases, and tiny particles that can get into the lungs.

Professional chefs will "prove" a new metal pan with oil before its first use. Pour cooking oil into the pan to a depth of about 0.8 inches, heat it up on the stove until very hot but not smoking;,pull to the side of the stove—or put it on the lowest heat possible—for at least six hours (overnight is ideal). Dispose of oil and wipe the pan out with a clean dry cloth.

Ideally, a metal frying pan should never be washed up. A wipe with a clean dry cloth should suffice. Any moisture will make food stick. To "prove" a moist pan with salt: cover its bottom with a thick layer of household salt; heat until the salt starts to turn brown and you can see residual water bubbling out of the metal. Dispose of salt and wipe pan out with a clean dry cloth.

THE MOST EXPENSIVE SECRET IN ROCK & ROLL

Cost TV executive Dick Ebersol $50,000 in August 2003. That's the donation he paid to a charity nominated by Carly Simon on condition she reveal to him the true identity of the man who inspired her 1972 hit, "You're So Vain." Ever since its release, speculation has run rife about the song's subject. Is it Warren Beatty? Kris Kristofferson? James Taylor? They were all at one time or another paramours to Ms. Simon, after all. For years, the rumor mill had a certain rock knight as the subject—and, coincidentally, one of the song's backing singers was Mick Jagger. But Carly had always kept schtum, until she revealed the subject to the curious Mr. Ebserol (who was under strict instructions to keep it to himself).

SECRET U.S. SOCIALIST PROPAGANDA

At the Coit Tower in San Francisco's Pioneer Park are a series of murals funded by the Works Progress Administration Federal Art Project, part of the Depression-era New Deal. Thousands of admirers come every year to see these frescoes of Californian agriculture and business life—but only those who look a little more closely can see evidence of the controversial story behind them. In 1933, the year before work started on the Coit Tower frescoes, a portrait of Lenin had been painted in that bastion of capitalism, the Rockefeller Center, by Mexican artist Diego Rivera. He was paid for the work, but the portrait was destroyed by the people who'd commissioned it, perhaps fearing the social message it contained. The outcry was immediate: across the U.S.A., artistic groups protested against the increasing censorship and repression they were experiencing. In support of Rivera, the artists involved in the Pioneer Park frescoes painted in clever touches as a rallying call to social protest and leftist reform. For example, on his mural newstands, Victor Arnoutoff painted left-wing publications *The Daily Worker* and *The New Masses*, while in a library scene painted by Bernard Zakheim, a man reaches for a volume of Karl Marx's *Das Kapital*. This was seen by the authorities as communist propaganda and they locked up Coit Tower for several months to protect the public until the dispute was resolved. Some people thought the offending sections of the murals should be whitewashed over, while others supported this creative example of free speech. In the end, only Clifford Wight's mural symbolizing the fight between capitalism and communism was obliterated—and posterity does not record who, when, or how this controversial whitewash was carried out. The other murals remain as a reminder of a secret artistic response to the anti-communism of the 1930s.

HIPPOCRATES'S SECRET

Everyone thinks that Hippocrates (460 to 377 B.C.) was the first known doctor, but over 2,000 years before, a Babylonian called Lulu was practicing as a medical professional in Sumer, in the southern part of modern-day Iraq. The first-known dentist was an Egyptian called Hesy-Re, who lived around 2,500 B.C. The first pharmacies or drugstores—selling herbs, alcohol, ointments, and perfumes—were set up throughout the Arabic world during the 9th century A.D.

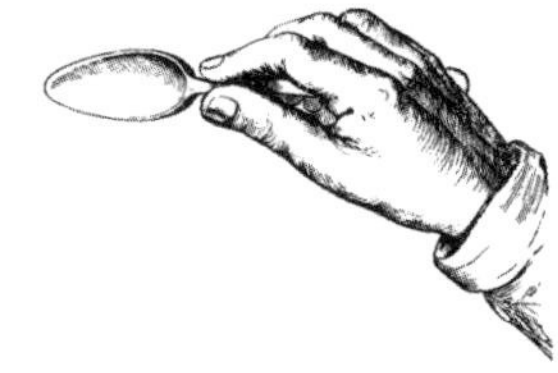

NIXON'S SECRET APOLLO 11 SPEECH

President Richard Nixon was prepared in the event of the Apollo 11 mission ending in catastrophe. His speechwriter William Safire drew up a text for the president to deliver in case Neil Armstrong and Edwin "Buzz" Aldrin were left stranded on the moon. "Fate has ordained that the men who went to the moon to explore in peace will stay on the moon to rest in peace. These brave men, Neil Armstrong and Edwin Aldrin, know that there is no hope for their recovery. But they also know that there is hope for mankind in their sacrifice . . ." To a shocked and grieving world, Nixon would have invoked the spirit of wonder and discovery represented by the astronauts: "In ancient days, men looked at stars and saw their heroes in the constellations. In modern times, we do much the same, but our heroes are epic men of flesh and blood . . ." The final words of the speech echoed the verse of Rupert Brooke, the English war poet. This time, however, the theme was not patriotism, but pride in humanity itself: "For every human being who looks up at the moon in the nights to come will know that there is some corner of another world that is forever mankind." Fortunately, the speech was never delivered and on 20 July 1969, Armstrong and Aldrin became the first men to walk on the moon.

THE SECRET OF THE TEMPLE SLOT MACHINE

The slot machine is supposed to have been invented in San Francisco in the 1890s by Charles Fey, who designed the Liberty Bell, a heavy, cast-iron machine. His slot machine was a gambling toy and clearly related to the metal boxes that line the casino aisles of Vegas today. However, slot machines—used for revenue-gathering rather than gambling purposes—were known as early as the first century A.D. The engineer and automata-maker Heron of Alexandria constructed the earliest-known example of a slot machine, which was used in temples. Before entering to worship everyone had to wash their face and hands. After putting a heavy, probably bronze, coin in the slot of Heron's machine, enough water would come out of the small tap on the front of it for a ritual hand and face wash. The gadget was based on a lever and valve system: the weight of the coin pushed down one end of a lever, the other end lifted a valve which allowed water to flow out. As the lever was lowered, the coin fell off, and the mechanism returned to its balanced position, shutting off the supply of water. The money in this ingenious invention would be regularly collected by the priests.

THE MANY SECRETS OF EGGS

Fresh eggs will have a rough, chalky texture to the outside of the shell; the older eggs are the smoother the shell will feel.

To determine the freshness of an egg, place it into a glass of water. If it lies down horizontally it is only a day or two old; if sits at a 45 degree angle it is between a week and 10 days old, and if it stands up vertically it is considerably older than that.

If you shake an egg and you can feel defined movement inside, then it is old. Because the moisture content of eggs diminishes over time, the contents shrink and the air pocket at the rounded ends expands.

When cracked and put in a pan, a fresh egg's yolk will stand up almost spherically and the proportion of thick white to thin white will be much greater. The older it is the more it will spread across the pan's surface.

If you are separating egg yolks and whites, use fresh eggs, because the membrane surrounding the yolk disintegrates with age and is far more likely to spill yolk into the white. If eggs are old, chill them before separating as the lower temperature will toughen the yolk's membrane.

Slightly older eggs are better for hard boiling—it is often difficult to remove shells from very fresh hard-boiled eggs.

Once you have taken hard-boiled eggs off the stove, place the saucepan under a running cold tap until the water is cold. This stops the eggs cooking in their own heat and prevents a greyish green ring from appearing around the yolks.

Very fresh eggs take longer to boil, so add an extra 30 seconds to what you would usually cook them for.

For total accuracy, many chefs use eggs by weight in recipes. As a rule of thumb the contents of a large egg weigh around 1.6 ounces and a medium egg about 1 ounce. About two thirds of an egg's weight is white, the remaining third is yolk.

Eggshells are porous. Storing eggs near anything with a strong aroma can taint their taste. Left in their cartons, the papier-mâchè will absorb anything.

Eggs will keep for several weeks in a cool room and be less susceptible to corrupting odors than in the fridge.

When cooked, the whites of eggs straight from the fridge will toughen far more than they would if they had been at room temperature. Remove from the fridge an hour before cooking.

When boiled, eggs straight from the fridge are likely to crack on contact with water. Use a small pan, leaving less scope for bumping about and cracking. A spoonful of vinegar in the water helps protect shells and stops the white leaking out if it does crack.

When thickening a hot liquid with eggs or egg yolks, add the liquid to the eggs in a bowl away from the stove to avoid separation or curdling. If you do have to add eggs to something being heated, do not stir raw eggs into boiling liquid as the egg will cook and harden before you can whisk it in. Let it cool slightly (to below 150 degrees F, as that's the temperature at which eggs coagulate) first.

If you have leftover egg whites, it's fine to freeze them.

A pinch of cream of tartar, added before you start whisking, will give egg white an extra lift and greater frothiness.

Egg whites have to be free from any corrupting substances if they are to be beaten to stiffness. Whisks and bowls should be clean and grease free, and any specks of yolk should be removed—either scooped out with the egg's shell or dabbed up with a dampened clean cloth.

Never beat egg whites in an aluminum bowl, it will turn them gray.

Do not cook, fry, or scramble eggs on a very high heat, as fast cooking causes egg whites to toughen.

For perfect scrambled eggs, always undercook them. It doesn't matter that they look far too runny in the pan—they will continue cooking in their own heat as you serve them.

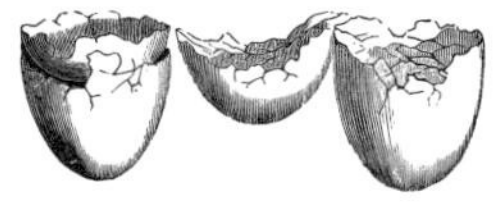

If scrambling eggs in a microwave, when you remove them and beat them during the process, always allow the bowl to stand for 30 seconds or so before continuing to cook. This will let the eggs cook in their own heat before you return them to the microwave and means you can more accurately judge the minimum time required for cooking, thus producing the fluffiest scrambled eggs.

THE SECRET OF ETERNAL YOUTH

"THE SECRET OF STAYING YOUNG IS TO LIVE HONESTLY, EAT SLOWLY, AND LIE ABOUT YOUR AGE."
Lucille Ball (*20th-century American comedienne*)

THE HUMANE SECRET OF THE GUILLOTINE

During the Terror of the French Revolution the guillotine was set up in the Place de la Révolution, now known as the Place de la Concorde in Paris, France. Thousands of Frenchmen—including Louis XVI and his Queen, Marie Antoinette—were decapitated there. But what's little known is that Dr. Joseph Ignace Guillotin, the man who gave his name to the guillotine, didn't actually invent this clinical contraption of death.

Today we think of the guillotine as a barbaric method of execution, but in those days it was considered a clean, efficient, and dignified way to die. When in 1789, as a member of the revolutionary Constituent Assembly, the humanitarian Dr. Guillotin suggested that decapitation by a beheading machine should become France's single method of execution, he was fighting for a more humane and egalitarian death penalty. At the time, only the rich and powerful could afford to pay for a quick execution by sword or axe rather than face the more usual and bloody torture of being hanged, drawn, and quartered, pulled to death by four oxen, or burnt at the stake. As a result of Dr. Guillotin's request, the guillotine we know today was drawn up and developed by Dr. Antoine Louis, secretary of the Surgical Academy.

During the Reign of Terror, the guillotine was variously called La Louisette or Le Louison (perhaps after Dr. Louis or indeed after Louis XVI himself), or nicknamed la Veuve (the widow) or "the national razor." It only became known as La Guillotine—in dubious honor of Dr. Guillotin—after the Reign of Terror was over.

Even in the 18th century, the guillotine was not a new method of execution, however. The English Halifax gibbet, an early version set up in the market place in Halifax, was used from at least 1280 to 1650, and possibly before; in Scotland, the "Maiden" was used from the 16th century and there is evidence that Ireland, Nuremberg, and Milan all had guillotines. But the French guillotine became a chilling symbol of the relentless horrors of the Reign of Terror. Dr. Guillotin himself escaped the use of the decapitation device that bears his name. He died of natural causes in 1814.

THE VOYNICH MANUSCRIPT

The Voynich Manuscript is an enduring enigma. An elaborately illustrated 246-page document dating from the later Middle Ages or Renaissance period, it is written in a language and script unlike any other. Wilfrid Voynich, a collector of rare books and manuscripts, said he discovered it in 1912 at a Jesuit college in Frascati, south-east of Rome, and attributed it to Roger Bacon, the 13th-century English Franciscan philosopher and pioneering scientist.

The mysteries of the manuscript do not end with its strange script. It features detailed drawings of plants that defy botanical classification, anatomical diagrams, astrological or astronomical wheels, and curious images of naked women sitting in tubs of green liquid.

Is it a secret religious text, written in code or a lost language? Is it the product of religious ecstasy, or perhaps mind-altering drugs? The efforts of historians, linguists, and cryptologists have yet to produce a convincing theory to explain the contents of the manuscript. Its resistance to interpretation has convinced many that it is simply a forgery. Some have identified Voynich as the author, but earlier candidates include the 16th-century English mathematician and occultist John Dee, or his medium Edward Kelley, a convicted counterfeiter. The Voynich Manuscript is now deposited at the Beinecke Rare Book and Manuscript Library at Yale University in Connecticut.

THE DESERT PLANT'S SECRET OF SURVIVAL

We expect a desert by definition to be a barren place. Apart from the odd oasis, which may sport a tall coconut tree or (in American deserts, certainly) a cactus or two, one does not expect to see much vegetation. But it is there, hidden from view.

In the deserts of South Africa where not much grows, any plant that dares to show its face is asking for trouble. In such a barren environment, if you are alive and green you will get eaten. So, if you are a plant at the bottom of the food chain like the Living Stone, you need a good disguise. Luckily, it has just that.

Short and very squat in a kind of browny-beige color, it looks just like a rock or a stone. Which, of course, is the perfect camouflage when you live in a desert full of stones. Problem solved.

BRITISH MILITARY UFO SECRETS

In the years after WWII, Royal Air Force crews and radar operators began reporting unidentified flying objects over England. Questions were asked at HQ over them. Were they highly advanced Russian aircraft or an attempt by extraterrestrial life forms to make contact with Earth? In the 1950s, the Ministry of Defence set up a special group, known as SF4, to investigate the strange phenomena.

They claimed that many of these early incidents were probably caused by teething troubles in the radar system and, as the technology developed, the number of occurrences on radar declined. However, there were still UFO sightings, often reported by seemingly reliable sources.

In 1976 the captain of a British Airways jet returning from Portugal reported seeing four bright objects—two cigar-shaped and two round—in the sky. A plane on the same flight path made a similar sighting later that night. In 1977, a Flight Lieutenant Wood reported that he'd observed luminous objects a few miles out at sea. His report was later corroborated by his colleagues.

On 27 December 1980, an incident occurred that has been hailed by ufologists as the British Roswell incident. Personnel at the U.S. Air Force base of Rendlesham in Suffolk reported seeing a hovering metallic object that was emitting light. The deputy base commander, Lt. Col. Charles Hart, who was off the site at the time, later took witness statements and compiled a dossier about the incident. Base personnel had found three depressions on the ground where the object had been seen and recorded low-levels of radiation around the depressions. However, unsurprisingly the Ministry of Defence treated the incident with scepticism from the outset. Their investigation concluded that the most likely source of the illumination was Orford Ness lighthouse, which is situated a few miles away.

The effect of the pulsating light coming through the nearby woods could have confused the base personnel, they argued. This explanation satisfied neither the U.S. military, nor the ufologists who suspected a cover-up—which would be completely in keeping with all previous incidents of suspected UFO sightings.

LONG ISLAND SOUND'S SECRET DEAD

Hart Island, off the shore of the Bronx in Long Island Sound, is where the city buries its unclaimed dead. During the Civil War the island was used to house Confederate prisoners, but since the late 1860s it has been the final resting place for New York's indigent and unknown. The cemetery is supervised by the Department of Corrections and prisoners from Riker's Island are ferried in each day from nearby City Island to work there. In the Second World War, Hart Island once again held prisoners of war, including the crew of a German U-boat captured nearby. In the mid-1950s a Nike surface-to-air missile battery was established on the island as a defense against Soviet attack. Although the base was closed in 1961, rendered obsolete by advances in military technology, many of the rusting facilities are still in place. The island is closed to the public.

SECRETS OF VIRAL MARKETING

A popular method of so-called "viral marketing" involves exploiting the relative anonymity of the Internet. Willing collaborators, some of them teenagers, are given free merchandise in return for flooding chat rooms and message boards with multiple rave reviews and detailed accounts of new films.

At the more creative end of the scale, those often subversive reworkings of current film posters that get sent around via email may well have started life in the marketing department of the film's studio.

THE SECRET OF BARGAIN HUNTING (FOOD)

Do end-of-day shopping. At closing time, many bakeries sell their produce at knocked-down prices. Fruit and vegetable sellers often do the same.

Don't shop on an empty stomach. As tempting as this sounds, it is never a good idea—you will spend on average between 17 and 20 percent more on your food groceries.

Don't shop with your children. Shopping with children adds around 30 percent to your normal grocery bill.

Be focused. In a supermarket, staple items are purposefully placed at the four corners of the store, meaning shoppers are more likely to go off-list. So don't be put off your predetermined course of shopping.

THE SECRET OF THOSE FOOTPRINTS AT GRAUMAN'S CHINESE THEATER

This landmark restaurant in Los Angeles is renowned for the foot and handprints made in the cement outside by the movie greats of Hollywood. Yet it wasn't a great feat of marketing that brought about the pavement full of prints.

It was an accident. The first stars officially to leave their mark were Mary Pickford and Douglas Fairbanks. But in fact actress Norma Talmadge established the tradition in 1927—when she stumbled into wet cement outside the newly-built theater by accident.

THE SECRET OF A PARIS TRAFFIC ISLAND

Nothing remains of Paris's infamous prison, the Bastille, a fortress whose storming on 14 July 1789 is still celebrated in France as marking the start of the Revolution. Despite legend (and numerous paintings of the event) depicting a scene of liberation for those imprisoned by the debauched ruling class, the revolutionary mob had been trying to seize the armaments and gunpowder stored there, and in fact only seven prisoners were actually liberated. Destruction of the hated prison began almost immediately, and by the end of November most of it had been demolished. An enterprising rogue named Palloy made models of the Bastille from its masonry, and sold them off as souvenirs. Between 1814 and 1846, a giant plaster elephant stood on the site. Napoleon had originally planned a triumphal arch there, but this was erected in the west of the city instead. Cautious of reviving revolutionary sentiment, Napoleon settled instead on the elephant, with its association of Carthage and imperial conquest. The site of one of the most momentous episodes in French history is now a traffic island.

CLEAN SECRETS

Clean the inside of a bottle with a spoonful of sand. Pour it into the bottle, add soapy water, shake vigorously, and empty out into a strainer. Thoroughly rinse the bottle and leave to dry. Dry and save the sand to use again.

Clean stained or tarnished roasting pans or enameled pots with meat tenderizer as it will break down the accumulated protein deposits.

SECRET BIG BANGERS

Since the end of the Second World War there have been 2,051 nuclear bomb tests around the world. There were 178 in 1962 alone. Countries that have been blasting are:

U.S.A. 1039	China 45
Russia (formerly Soviet Union) 718	India...3
France 198	Pakistan 2
United Kingdom 45	Unknown (rather worryingly)..........1

INTERPRETING THE SECRETS OF THE GODS IN ANCIENT GREECE

An oracle was a shrine in which the gods revealed secret knowledge of their divine purpose to mortals. The most celebrated was the oracle of Apollo at Delphi on the slopes of Mount Parnassus, which dates back to the 7th century B.C. After the supplicant had paid a contribution, they would consult the oracle in the inner shrine, where the stone that the ancient Greeks believed was the center of the world stood. The oracular prophecy was delivered by the Pythia, a local woman aged over 50, who lived as a virgin during her time in office. Prior to a consultation, she would bathe in the sacred Castalian spring before making burnt offerings and entering her cell, where she sat on a tripod crowned with laurel, the sacred tree of Apollo. Inspired by the god, she would make her pronouncement, which was interpreted by the oracle priests. The answers given were usually ambiguous, but this didn't prevent statesmen from bringing serious questions about the course of war or political action to the oracle.

At the oracle of Zeus at Dodona, the priests interpreted the rustling of the leaves on a sacred oak. Other oracles used incubation, where the enquirer slept in a sacred grotto and the answer was revealed to them in a dream.

THE SECRET LIFE OF THE BOND THEME

The best-known film theme of all time has to be Monty Norman's "James Bond Theme." But it wasn't written for Bond. It began life as a tune called "Bad Sign, Good Sign," which Norman had written as a sitar instrumental for an unproduced stage production of V. S. Naipaul's *A House For Mr. Biswas*.

CHELSEA HOTEL SECRETS

The Chelsea Hotel, on West 23rd Street near the corner of 7th Avenue, is possibly the only commercial travelers' inn to have its own published Manifesto. The hotel is celebrated as the haunt of the bohemian and creative, boasting a guest list that has included Mark Twain, Sarah Bernhardt, Vladimir Nabokov, and Dylan Thomas. However it was artist Yves Klein who, in 1961 while a long-term guest at the Chelsea, wrote the Chelsea Hotel Manifesto and published it to coincide with his first one-man show.

In the Manifesto he makes extraordinary statements—that birds must be eliminated, for instance—or nonsensical but intellectually challenging irrelevancies such as: "Jonathan Swift, in his Voyage to Laputa (*Gulliver's Travels*), gave the distances and periods of rotation of two satellites of Mars though they were unknown at the time; when American astronomer, Asaph Hall, discovered them in 1877, he realized that his measurements were the same as those of Swift. Seized by panic, he named them Phobos and Deimos, Fear and Terror!" The Manifesto is understood to be memorized by various long-term hotel residents.

Originally built in 1884 as an apartment building, the Chelsea was for 18 years the tallest (12 stories) building in New York. Initially conceived as a co-operative, it went bankrupt in 1903 and became a hotel in 1905. After Mark Twain made it his home in New York, scores of writers and artists made their way there. In the mid-1960s Bob Dylan wrote "Sad-Eyed Lady of the Lowlands" in the hotel, and it inspired Joni Mitchell's "Chelsea Morning" and Nico's "Chelsea Girl." Andy Warhol used various apartments in the hotel for his entourage, and Leonard Cohen's song "Chelsea Hotel No. 2" was an account of a sexual encounter with Janis Joplin in Room 104. It was later the setting of punk tragedy. On 12 October 1978, Sid Vicious of the Sex Pistols is thought to have murdered his American girlfriend Nancy Spungen in Room 100 of the hotel. He took a fatal heroin overdose in New York the following February while on bail for the killing.

CHURCHILL'S SECRET BUNKER

During the wartime bombing of London, British Prime Minister Winston Churchill governed from underground Cabinet War Rooms in Whitehall. However, an alternative secret bunker, codenamed Paddock, was constructed in Dollis Hill in north-west London. This two-story bunker under Brook Road was completely bombproof and designed to accommodate 200 cabinet and staff members. It was to have been used as a last resort in the event of a German invasion. Churchill stayed there once but apparently didn't find it to his taste.

A trip to Dollis Hill today will reveal how the ground level site above has been developed into houses, but there are still two secret entrances to the listed bunker: one via a discreet steel door in a wall between two houses, and the other through a one-story brick building.

In central London, there were several other, smaller fortified bunkers built in the 1930s. These are to be found under Curzon Street in Mayfair, at Montague House in Whitehall, at Storey's Gate, in Horseferry Road, and on Horseguards Parade. None of which ever hosted an evening with Winston Churchill.

THE SECRET HISTORY OF THE PARIS COMMUNE

When the subject of May Revolutions in Paris comes up, people usually think of the year 1968. But almost a century before then, Paris underwent a real revolution in which the city was controlled not by the usual authorities, but by the people, for the people.

Père-Lachaise in the French capital is the most famous cemetery in Paris and probably the world. The graves are a "who's who" of French artistic and cultural history and there is also room for celebrated foreigners such as Oscar Wilde and Jim Morrison. However it is also the scene of the death of the first-ever workers' revolution, called the Paris Commune.

From 18 March to 28 May in 1871, Parisian workers took over the city. But this popular, egalitarian movement could not last long against the troops of the French government who attacked Paris, killing between 17,000 and 30,000 Commune supporters in just one week.

The last 150 revolutionaries were eventually cornered in the south-eastern edge of Père-Lachaise, where government troops lined them up and shot them. The wall, now known as the Mur des Fédéres or Wall of Federalists, has been preserved, complete with the bullet holes.

THE SECRET OF LIFE

"THE SECRET OF LIFE IS HONESTY AND FAIR DEALING. IF YOU CAN FAKE THAT, YOU'VE GOT IT MADE."
Groucho Marx (*20th-century American comedian*)

"PART OF THE SECRET OF A SUCCESS IN LIFE IS TO EAT WHAT YOU LIKE AND LET THE FOOD FIGHT IT OUT INSIDE."
Mark Twain (*19th-century American author*)

THE SECRETS OF SUCCESSFUL PERSUASION

Marketing gurus know there are a number of psychologically based marketing tricks guaranteed to make consumers buy things they don't need. But why leave these secrets to the boardroom? Translate the following golden rules of persuasion into every part of your life, and watch your influence soar.

CREATE AN ILLUSION OF SCARCITY.

This encourages a sense of urgency prompting people to act quicker—and therefore more impulsively—than they usually would. It also creates an impression of exclusivity since the snob-factor adds instant value.

APPRECIATE THE POWER OF RECIPROCITY.

The theory here is that when someone gives you something of perceived value, you immediately want to give something back, however subconscious that feeling may be. For instance, a shampoo sample free with a magazine will incite a customer to pick that new shampoo when next faced with a pharmacist shelf.

DEMONSTRATE AUTHORITY.

People want the best and the ultimate, so create the impression that what you are pushing is just that. This authority can be an illusion. Studies show shops that play classical music find it easier to sell more expensive items than ones playing pop music; customers automatically feel more refined. Consider commitment and consistency. Stability and reliability may not be the sexiest of qualities, but since both generate trust, they are ultimately invaluable. ❀

ABANDONED NEW YORK SUBWAY STATIONS #5

MYRTLE AVENUE AND DE KALB AVENUE

LOCATION: AT MYRTLE AVE., DE KALB AVE., AND FLATBUSH AVE.

OPENED IN JUNE 1915 AND CLOSED IN JULY 1956.

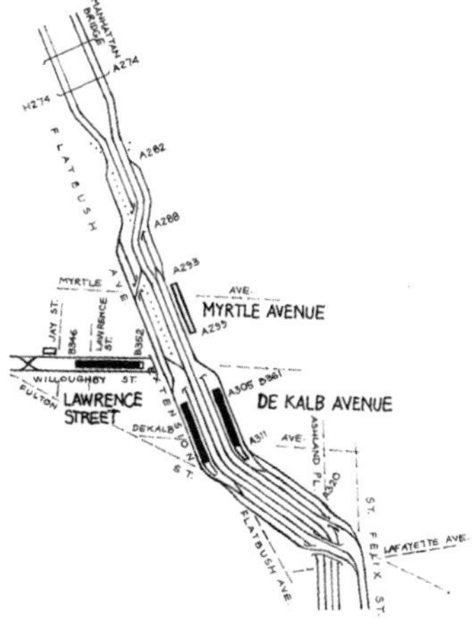

A part of the same Manhattan Bridge Dual System (originally called the Brooklyn Loop Line) as De Kalb Avenue Station (opened June 1915, closed 1960). Myrtle Avenue was a local stop in the middle of the Expressway and originally planned (in 1908) to have five tracks. De Kalb was to have six. However, as the subway system was redrawn and developed, things changed. Eventually four tracks would run through Myrtle Avenue and despite a plan for the Myrtle Ave. El to be above the subway station, after Flatbush Avenue was extended over it in 1909 those plans were dropped. Many people consider the failure to build the elevated station there one of the major missed opportunities of the New York Transit system. De Kalb proved to be a serious choke point for the subway system and in 1956 a major rebuild of the area began. Myrtle was bypassed, its southbound platform removed and the northbound left but abandoned. By 1960 many of the De Kalb platforms had also become obsolete. Since 1980 Myrtle Avenue has been home to a piece of installation art by Bill Brand. Originally designed to be an animated cartoon, it has long since ceased to move and is almost obliterated by dirt and graffiti.

THE SECRETS OF YOUR DAILY BREAD

Baking a loaf of bread using traditional methods—mixing, proving, kneading, proving, and baking—takes approximately four hours. Modern bread "factories" have reduced this time to around 40 minutes.

※ ※ ※

Commercially produced bread can have the highest salt content of all our everyday foods, as 0.02 ounces of salt per 3.5 ounces of bread is not uncommon. The reason for this is because salt provides flavor that the accelerated manufacturing time does not allow to develop naturally.

※ ※ ※

Most factory-baked brown bread is exactly that: brown, rather than actually wholemeal. Bizarrely, standard commercial brown bread starts life as white bread, which is bread with the bits of the grain that would make the flour brown taken out, then this newly-whitened flour is dyed brown. The reason for this is to get rid of the coarser texture caused by those bits of grain, but retain the illusion of the bread still having the healthy properties they would bring to it.

※ ※ ※

Thanks to the modern bakery industry, livestock is getting better nourished than we are from the majority of bread consumed. When the wheat grain is milled—crushed into flour—the brown bran (the husk) and the germ (from which the new plant will grow) are discarded to leave the white flour for bakery use. The bran contains the grain's fiber and some of the mineral content, while the germ hosts oils, all the vitamins, and most of the minerals, yet these are sold off to animal feed companies as surplus to mass-produced bread's requirements.

※ ※ ※

Supermarket "in-store bakeries" are little more than smoke and mirrors to get us a) thinking about buying bread, and b) assuming all the food on offer is fresh and somehow wholesome. That bread is as "baked on the premises" as the finish-off-in-the-oven pre-packaged loaves you would buy off their shelves. It's shipped in from the big factories pre-prepared up to the point it needs browning off in an oven, which is the only part of the process that will take place on the supermarket branch's premises.

※ ※ ※

Beware of reading the words "flour," "treatment," and "agent" in that order on a loaf of bread's label. They are industry shorthand for a range of chemicals, oxidants, enzymes, and even hydrogenated fat, which, as they are there to assist the process rather than be part of the finished result, don't have to be declared individually on the packaging or label. None of these ingredients are there to make the bread taste better or be better for you, the consumer.

※ ※ ※

Don't be fooled by any Vitamin C content being trumpeted on a loaf's label. It is a cunning way of describing ascorbic acid, the only oxidizing agent now permitted by law. An oxidizing agent is necessary in modern bread production, in order to get the required amount of air in to make the dough rise so rapidly and fluffily. Before ascorbic acid, bread manufacturers used potassium bromide, which had the useful side effect of bleaching the flour an even brighter shade of white.

※ ※ ※

In bread manufacture, both hydrogenated fat and fractionated fat may merely be described as "vegetable fat" or, in the case of the latter, "palm oil."

※ ※ ※

One of the main causes of increased coliac disease or gluten allergy in modern times is the introduction of flour with a super-high gluten content into mass-produced bread, as it needs those levels to give it the strength to survive the factory baking process. It is also this extra gluten that makes modern bread so chewy.

SECRETS OF UNDERCOVER MARKETING

In the 1950s when television became a mass market medium the idea of advertisements was considered new, of course, but it was also considered something of a service to the public. Ads were designed to offer labor-saving devices to the hard working mothers of America, and they were filmed to look as much like a mini movie as possible. Salesmen and women were friendly types with open faces and winning smiles. The message that they were selling was clear and obvious. Forty years later, however, the public was showing distinct signs of advertising fatigue. Obvious "sells" were derided as cheap and exploitative. The public stopped buying into ads. Something had to be done, and so it was. A generation of smart young people in the early 1990s started developing new and subtle ways to sell us things that we didn't need or want in none-to-obvious ways. In the 21st century, advertisers are finding ever more ingenious ways of relieving us of our money. A relatively recent method is "undercover" or "stealth" marketing, whereby the consumer is targeted without knowing it. Such targeting often occurs where the consumer's guard is down, in a bar, perhaps, or a coffee shop. Attractive young people are hired to appear absorbed with a particular product, or to offer to buy their neighbor a cool new drink they have discovered. The curiosity of those around them is provoked and before long the consumer thinks the drink is pretty cool too, and they are asking the company's representative for information—information the planted people are only too willing to provide.

This is a controversial way of going about your business, of course, but companies who have employed such techniques claim that those polled did not have a problem with being sold to in this way. ⌛

WE CAN SEE YOU, MR. BOND

One would assume that the headquarters of Britain's secret services would be, somehow, secret. Yet since 1995 the Headquarters of MI5, the British Security Service, have been openly located at Thames House, 11 Millbank. Previously, it had been based on Curzon Street, and before that at 140 Gower Street, nicknamed "Russia House."

Further upstream on the other side of the river is Vauxhall Cross, the new headquarters of MI6, the Secret Intelligence Service. It was "blown up" in the opening scenes of the 1999 James Bond film *The World Is Not Enough*. The movie and, therefore, MI6 headquarters were shown widely around the world, making them a very badly kept secret.

THE SECRET OF REMEMBERING NAMES

Picture the scene. You're at a party talking to an acquaintance, wracking your brain trying to remember their name, all the while delaying introducing them to anyone else in case you're found out. What's the one thing worse than someone forgetting your name? Suffering the embarrassment of forgetting someone else's. So here are some secret methods to ensure you will never, ever find yourself in that toe-curling situation again.

PAY CAREFUL ATTENTION TO THE NAME WHEN YOU ARE INTRODUCED TO SOMEONE.

Say his or her name to yourself again. Then try and bring it into the ensuing conversation as much as possible to reinforce your memory. This will also ensure you are pronouncing their name correctly.

DON'T BE AFRAID TO ASK HOW TO SPELL A DIFFICULT NAME.

If you know the spelling, you can picture this in your mind and you should remember it better. Once alone, write down the new name several times, all the while picturing the person's face.

PAINT A PICTURE.

Visual images are powerful memory tools. If you meet someone called Rachel Moss, for instance, imagine her sitting on a mossy knoll.

TRY MAKING UP A RHYME.

Rhyming is an excellent way to boost the memory—why else do you think they are so effective for teaching children? If you meet a Jane who looks plain, you won't forget.

LINK A NAME WITH A PERSON'S PROFESSION.

"Phil does ills," for instance, might help you recall the name of a medical doctor.

THINK OF A WORD ASSOCIATION.

If you meet a Mr. Auld, who is old, hold that thought.

And finally, if all the above fails and you draw a blank, lure someone else—whose name you remember—into the conversation. Say, perhaps, "I'd like you to meet my friend X." The other person should then introduce him or herself. ❀

THE SECRETS OF AZTEC HUMAN SACRIFICE

The Aztecs carried out human sacrifice on a scale unparalleled in any other society. The Aztec capital Tenochtitlán, razed by Cortes in 1521, was on the site of modern-day Mexico City. The center of the city was dominated by a 100 ft. high pyramid, on which stood the temples of Huitzilopochtli and Tlaloc, the gods of war and rain. On top were altars on which four priests would hold down sacrificial victims while their hearts were cut out. The idea was to nourish the god by offering a living human heart—the braver the victim, the more thankful the god would be. The bodies were then thrown down the side of the temple, sometimes to be cooked and eaten by the priests or people.

Thousands of human sacrifices were carried out, mostly on prisoners captured in war. But the most celebrated Aztec sacrifice was that of a handsome youth who was chosen each year to impersonate the god Tezcatlipoca. For one year he would live a life of luxury and honor, and be worshipped as an embodiment of the god. At the end of the period, he would climb the temple, symbolically smashing the clay flutes he had played throughout the year, before having his heart cut out.

SECRET "ASSASSINS"

The word "assassin" is taken from the Arabic for "user of hashish," and was originally used in the West to describe a fearsome, secret order of the Ismaili sect of Islam which emerged during the 11th-century power struggle within the Fatimid dynasty.

The Assassins—much like Al Qaeda today—were renowned for their secrecy, discipline, and the adoption of religious terrorism.

Their name referred to their supposed practice of smoking marijuana to conjure up the visions of paradise that would inspire them to martyrdom.

However it has been pointed out that extensive smoking of, or eating hashish is hardly likely to imbue the inhaler with the necessary nerves of steel that would be considered requisite to carry out an assassination. Indeed it is likely that the so-called assassin would forget whatever mission he was sent on and look for some sweet dates to eat instead.

It is more likely that the name was adopted by the sect in order to make themselves sound more fearsome, committed, and frightening than they were. Thus they gained their reputation.

A SECRET WINE CELLAR AT WHITEHALL

Under the Whitehall headquarters or "Main Building" of the Ministry of Defence in London is a vaulted wine cellar that dates back to the Tudor period. The building was originally part of the residence of Cardinal Wolsey, the 16th-century churchman who dominated the early years of Henry VIII's reign.

The 70 ft. by 30 ft. cellar survived the fire that ravaged Whitehall in 1698, although afterwards Sir Christopher Wren was asked by the Board of Green Cloth, who managed household affairs, to repair some roof leaks, for "The wine lodged therein may receive much damage if timely care be not taken." In 1949, the whole cellar was encased in a protective cocoon of steel and concrete and moved 40 ft. on rollers, to allow a steel frame to be attached to it. The vaulted structure was then moved intact back into the basement of the Main Building, where it remains to this day.

GLENN MILLER: SECRET WEAPON

On 30 October 1944, Glenn Miller and his U.S. Air Force band recorded a special session at the Abbey Road studios in London. These recordings were made for the American Broadcast Station in Europe and the intended audience was the German military; in other words, Glenn Miller's tunes were to be a subtle secret weapon in the wars for hearts and minds. The band was referred to as "A true symbol of America, where everybody has the same rights. It is equal regardless of race, color, and religion." The session was introduced in German by the bandleader himself, helped by translator Ilse Weinberger. Some of the band's standards were sung in German by vocalist Johnny Desmond. The band recorded enough music that day for six programs, which were cheekily transmitted over the airwaves as "Music for the Wehrmach."

E SECRETS

E Numbers are the European Union codings given to various food additives. They were first introduced in 1983 to provide an easy reference for consumers. They are present in most processed foods to enhance (or even create) flavor depleted by the manufacturing process, and to extend the food's shelf life by stopping it going bad so quickly. They can also be for purely aesthetic purposes, to make a food look more like the popular image of it. Although some E numbers occur naturally—E440 is pectin; or E330, citric acid—90 percent serve no nutritional purpose at all.

Within 10 years of their introduction listing, E numbers on a product's label began to put potential buyers off. As a result they appear to have all but disappeared from processed food. But they are still there, they are simply disguised. As long as they are listed they are complying with European Union regulations, thus they are now displayed by name rather than E number coding. For example, Benzoic Acid is still E210, and it's still dangerous to asthma sufferers, but it's less likely to be noticed when named rather than numbered. There are also a couple of legal loopholes that further mask the presence of E numbers. If an additive is used as a "processing aid," which means it's been used to make the food rather than as an actual ingredient, then it doesn't have to be listed as an ingredient. Many of these processing aids will leave behind undesirable traces. "Compounding" is when an E number has been used as an ingredient in something that has been pre-prepared to go into the final food—for instance the jam in a factory-manufactured tart only has to be listed as "jam," and not broken down into the ingredients that went into it.

Some popularly used additives that should be avoided, by name and number:

COLORINGS

BROWN HT, E155, BROWN; CARMOISINE, E122, RED; POCEAU, E124, RED; SUNSET YELLOW, E120, YELLOW; TARTRAZINE, E102, YELLOW
Should all be avoided by people allergic to aspirin, as they could trigger skin rashes or upset stomachs; also may cause asthmatics to experience breathing difficulties.

ERYTHROSINE, E127, RED
Could increase thyroid hormone levels to overactivity.

BLACK PN, E151, BLACK
Can cause cysts.

INDIGO CARMINE, E132, BLUE; PATENT BLUE, E131, BLUE
Can both set off existing allergies, immediately.

PRESERVATIVES

SORBIC ACID, E200
Can cause skin irritation.

BENZOIC ACID, E210; CALCIUM BENZOATE, E213; ETHYL PARA-HYDROXYBENOATE, E214; METHYL P ZARA-HYDROXYBENOATE, E218; POTASSIUM BENZOATE, E212; SODIUM BENZOATE, E211; SODIUM PARA-HYDROXYBENOATE, E215
Can cause intestinal irritation and possible mouth-numbing, asthmatics are particularly susceptible.

POTASSIUM ACETATE, E261
To be avoided by anybody with kidney problems.

POTASSIUM AND SODIUM NITRITES, E249 AND E250
Can destroy red blood corpuscles, reduce the amount of oxygen in the blood and lower blood pressure. Have carcinogenic potential.

SULPHUR DIOXIDE, E220
Causes gastric irritation, destroys the Vitamin E content of flour.

ALL SULPHITES, E221-227
Can cause gastric upset and will reduce the vitamin content of food they are added to. Particularly dangerous to asthmatics.

HEXAMINE, E239
Causes the body to internally produce formaldehyde.

SODIUM AND POTASSIUM NITRATE, E251-252
Although essential to prevent toxicity occurring in meat, these have the potential to convert into nitrites in the stomach.

ANTIOXIDANTS

PROPHYL GALLATE, E310; OCTYL GALLATE, E311; DODECYL GALLATE E312
Can cause intestinal irritation if ingested by asthma sufferers or those allergic to aspirin.

BUTYLATED HYDROXYANISOLE (BHA), E320
Can raise LDL cholesterol levels, and inhibit the body's absorption of vitamins.

BUTYLATED HYDROXYTOLENE (BHA), E321
Can cause skin rashes and inhibit the body's absorption of vitamins.

THE SECRET OF THE AMBER ROOM

The greatest art mystery of the post-war period was the disappearance of the fabled Amber Room at the Catherine Palace at Tsarskoye Selo in Russia. Hailed in the 18th century as the eighth wonder of the world, the exquisite amber-paneled chamber had been the centerpiece of Catherine the Great's favorite residence, about 15 miles outside St. Petersburg. In 1941, as the German forces closed in on Leningrad, as the city was then called, the decision was made to evacuate important works of art to Siberia. However, the Amber Room proved too delicate to move and instead was concealed behind wall coverings. This disguise was unsuccessful and after German troops overran the palace, the room was dismantled and packed off to a castle in Königsberg (modern-day Kaliningrad) in East Prussia. After the war ended, the Soviet authorities sought to bring back the Amber Room, but it had disappeared. Over the years, the room became a Holy Grail for the historians who searched for it and a propaganda tool for the Russians, righteously aggrieved at the looting of their artistic treasures. The Amber Room was variously thought to be in cellars in Potsdam, Nazi bunkers, and at one stage hidden in the depths of the Nicolai Stollen mine on the German-Czech border.

However, new evidence suggests that the Amber Room did not survive the war. In fact, it appears to have been destroyed by the actions of the Red Army, rather than the Germans. At the end of the war, Russian troops occupied the castle in Königsberg in which it was stored and, in an atmosphere of looting and casual destruction, it seems likely the room was destroyed by fire. Embarrassed by the Amber Room's fate and their own failure to protect it, this fact was covered up by Soviet investigators. The fruitless search for the Amber Room also proved politically useful, a counterbalance to German claims for the return of their stolen artworks. A replica of the Amber Room was unveiled in 2003 as part of the celebrations of the tercentenary of the founding of St. Petersburg.

THE BROOKLYN BRIDGE'S SECRET CURSE

Designed by the German-born John A. Roebling, this great example of 19th-century engineering spans the East River from Manhattan Island to Brooklyn. It is used by thousands every day to get in and out of Manhattan and is considered one of the great symbols of NYC. Yet to its creators, this bridge carried a curse. In 1869, as building work began, Roebling was fatally wounded after his foot was crushed by a ferry. He contracted tetanus and died soon after. His son, Washington Roebling, took over the project, but was crippled in 1872 after suffering the bends as he returned too rapidly from the underwater excavation chambers below the bridge. The bridge was opened to the public in 1893. Two years later, R. E. Odlum became the first man to jump from the bridge—and died from the fall.

THE SPIDER CRAB'S SURVIVAL SECRET

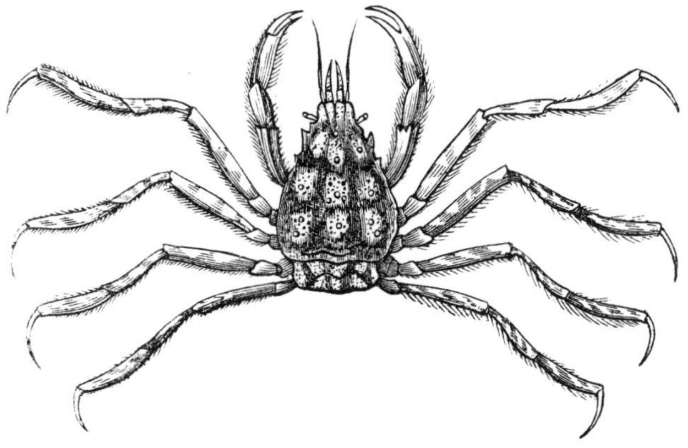

The spider crab's disguise is perfect. It makes use of the hook-like hairs covering its shell and legs to attach algae and other detritus from the seabed to its body, including the odd sea anemone. With its living camouflage jacket, whether on the move or lying doggo in the sand or silt, the spider crab is indistinguishable from the seabed.

SECRET LOTIONS AND POTIONS

Wheatgrass may be something of a magic potion when it comes to detoxing and cleansing the system, and, apparently, reducing the effects of aging. But unless it is consumed within 15 minutes of juicing it won't have any effect as the high chlorophyll content evaporates.

Don't wash your daily vitamin supplements down with your morning cup of tea or coffee, as it will block many of the vitamins and minerals being absorbed into your system. Likewise, large amounts of tea and coffee can affect a person's overall levels of nutrient intake.

Creatine is marketed as something of a miracle healer and memory booster, but heavy use can play havoc with our digestion—which is why professional athletes have named it "Creatine havoc."

Prolonged exposure to fluorescent lighting can set off a chemical reaction that will drastically deplete many fruit and vegetables' nutrient levels.

Much is made of green tea and red wine's antioxidant content (antioxidants inhibit cell deterioration that can lead to cancer and the visible effects of aging), but by far the best source is cocoa powder. Serving for serving, top quality cocoa powder will have around three times the antioxidant properties of green tea and even more than that of red wine.

In China, shiitake mushrooms are seen as the secret to a long life; in the western world research has shown them to lower LDL (bad) cholesterol levels and even be effective in halting advanced cancers.

Turmeric is very good in combatting the sort of scalp problems that may lead to hair loss.

A GENIUS'S SECRET

"THE SECRET OF GENIUS IS TO CARRY THE SPIRIT OF THE CHILD INTO OLD AGE, WHICH MEANS NEVER LOSING YOUR ENTHUSIASM."
Aldous Huxley (*20th-century British author*)

THE SECRET HISTORY OF FIREWORKS

The ancient Chinese used fireworks at celebrations such as New Year, weddings, or the birth of children because they believed the loud bangs would scare off evil spirits and ensure good fortune. The sole purpose of these early fireworks was to make as much noise as possible, and it was later that other chemicals were added to produce different colored explosions.

※ ※ ※

Handel's explosive "Music For The Royal Fireworks" was commissioned by King George I in 1716 to celebrate the signing of a peace treaty with Austria.

※ ※ ※

In fireworks manufacture, the basic chemical powders added to the gunpowder to create different colored explosions are (subtler shades are created by blending them):

Red........................Strontium nitrate
Orange.....................................Iron
Green........Chlorate or barium nitrate
Yellow.................................Sodium
Blue....................................Copper
White ....Magnesium or aluminium

A SECRET TEMPLE

Europe is littered with temples built for different religions, sects, and secret societies. One of the oddest is the temple to the mysterious cult of Mithras in the basement of a residential block behind the Circus Maximus in Rome.

Mithra was an Indo-Iranian god of light, but in the 2nd and 3rd centuries A.D, his cult began to spread in the Roman world, perhaps as a pagan backlash against the new religion of Christianity. Only men could be admitted to the cult, which revolved around the sacrifice of a bull. After a secret initiation ceremony, members would work their way up through a series of seven hierarchical grades, each of which had astrological symbolism including the Raven (ruled by Mercury), Soldier (Mars), Lion (Jupiter), and finally the Pater (father, ruled by Saturn) who could head his own congregation.

The cult of Mithras was never fully accepted by the Romans and its ceremonies and activities remain tantalizingly secret, but it is thought that it was popular with those in the armies, freedmen, and slaves. The temple would have been underground at the time that it was built and in use.

HEALTH FOOD SECRETS

Three dried apricots contain the same amount of iron as the average iron tablet, and the apricots won't give you constipation.

It's not just green vegetables that protect against cancer. Along with broccoli, cabbage, spring greens, kale, and watercress, the root vegetables turnips, radishes, and swede are all rich in antioxidant phytochemicals, which protect against cancers.

"Bad diet" is the most common factor in cases of every major disease in humans.

Sage oil supplements are a better memory aid than ginko or ginseng.

Vitamin C can protect you against passive smoking, so drink a fresh tomato or orange juice before you spend the evening in a smoky bar.

Up to a third of cases of cancer could be avoided by increased fresh fruit and vegetables in the daily diet.

Very few of us drink enough water: 12 and a half cups per day for a man; 8 and a half cups per day for a woman. When you feel hungry, you may well be thirsty and your body is telling you your water levels are dropping. When you start to feel thirsty, your internal water levels are getting worryingly low.

Portion for portion sushi is probably the most nutritious food there is. Seaweed is loaded with potassium and iron, the fish will have the maximum amount of Omega-3 fatty acids and be rich in protein, and the other vegetables are high fiber.

Dandelion leaves lower blood pressure, stimulate the liver, and reduce cholesterol levels. They can be eaten in salads or taken as a supplement.

Vegetarians, on average, live longer than those who eat meat. Adolf Hitler was a vegetarian.

Children should not eat the same foods as adults, as they need more calories and all-round nutrition than adults. Reduced-fat foods such as milk or cheese should be substituted for their full fat counterparts for growing children, and the high fiber plans that can help adults can harm a very young digestive system.

Don't peel potatoes—use them in their skins for mash and fries as well as roasting, boiling, and baking. Not only will they taste better but most nutrients are held just below the skin and by peeling them the goodness ends up in the trashcan.

THE SECRET OF SURVIVAL FOR EUROPEAN CATS

If a cat wishes to live a privileged and long life, then it should move to the Eternal City. Rome is home to an estimated population of 300,000 stray cats. Fed by a legion of *gattare* or cat ladies (once including the Italian film star Anna Magnani) they are a common sight among the ruins in the city. The cats enjoy considerable protection under local law, including the right to remain wherever they were born. At the Largo Argentina archaeological site, not far from where Julius Caesar was assassinated, a cat sanctuary provides food and veterinary care for thousands of animals, supported by local fund-raising and donations from the London-based Anglo-Italian Society for the Protection of Animals.

ABANDONED NEW YORK SUBWAY STATIONS #6

SEDGWICK AVENUE

LOCATION: AT THE FOOTBRIDGE OVER SEDGWICK AVENUE AND MAJOR DEEGAN EXPRESSWAY

OPENED JULY 1918, CLOSED AUGUST 1958.

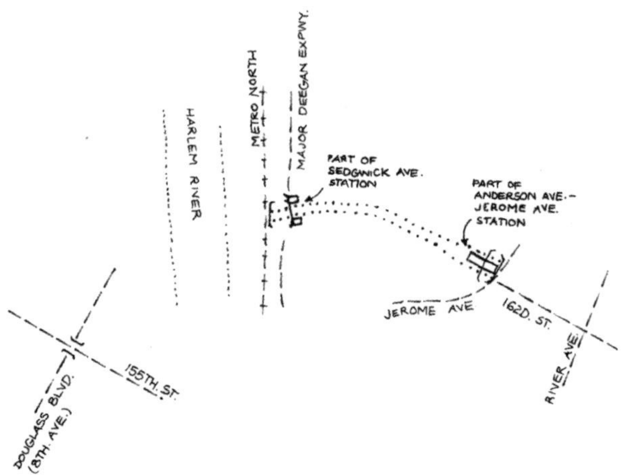

Originally part of an "underground el," Sedgwick Ave. station was mostly at ground level with concrete platforms on each side of the two tracks. The west end was a wood platform on a steel structure passing over the New York Central's Hudson Division. The east end was in a tunnel for about a car length. As part of the Dual System planned in 1913, the IRT built an extension of the joint 6 Ave. and 9 Ave. els from 155 St. and 8 Ave. Manhattan, to join the city's Jerome Ave. route. The extension routed the el over the railroad's Putnam Bridge, and the railroad was cut back to a new terminal on the Bronx side called Sedgwick Ave., where there had not been a station before. The IRT blasted a tunnel for three blocks and then continued the line by el to meet the city's Jerome Ave. line at 162 St., over River Ave. When the City took control of the joint Subway and el trains in 1940, it closed several els, including 9 Street. The tunnel remained open mostly for the Polo Grounds. When Putnam closed in 1958, the steel elevated section was removed. Today the remains of the station can be seen under the Major Deegan Expressway.

THE SECRET BOND BOY

The 1981 James Bond movie *For Your Eyes Only* was in many ways the usual mix of cars, girls, gloriously implausible plotlines, and gadgets, but this movie had a difference: one of the actresses proud to call herself "girl at pool" had once upon a time been a guy. Caroline Cossey's sex-change operation had taken place in 1974, although she had changed her name to Caroline in 1972. Several years after the operation she embarked on a successful modeling career and was cast in the Bond movie in 1980.

After two failed attempts at marriage—one was not allowed because she was still male in the eyes of English law, the other was annulled after her husband left her not long after the honeymoon—she wrote two books and resumed her modeling career. She is now married to a Canadian named David Finch. ⌛

THE SECRET OF *CASABLANCA*'S ALTERNATE ENDING

One of the most popular movies of all time, *Casablanca* began life when playwright Murray Burnett visited the cabaret "La Belle Aurure" in Cap Ferrat during the summer of 1938. He fashioned a play which he called *Everybody Comes To Rick's*. The Studio who would make the movie of the play, Warner Bros., changed the title.

There has been a wealth of rumors attached to the film over the years. For instance, despite persistent rumors to the contrary, Ronald Reagan was never the original choice for the role of Rick, although he was considered for the role of Victor Laszlo. George Raft *was* suggested for Rick, but eventually the role went to Humphrey Bogart, of course, who at that time was hot off *The Maltese Falcon*. Ann Sheridan (*Angels With Dirty Faces*; *The Man Who Came To Dinner*) and Hedy Lamarr (*Algiers*; *White Cargo*) were both considered for the role of Ilsa before it went to Ingrid Bergman.

There have long been stories of an alternate ending to the film and there almost was one. In light of the Allied landings at Casablanca, which took place just prior to the film's opening, studio bosses argued for a final scene showing Bogart and Claude Rains on board a ship, listening to a patriotic speech by President Roosevelt. Fortunately, producer Hal Wallis insisted on the now classic shot of Bogart remarking to Rains, as they stroll off into the fog: "Louis, I think this is the beginning of a beautiful friendship." 🔔

THE SECRETS OF GIVING FLOWERS #2

When giving a love roses, according to the Victorians, the following held a secret message:

A single rosebud
I love you

Red rosebud
you are young and beautiful

Red rose in full bloom
I still love you

Full-blown rose above two buds
this must remain a secret

A single white rose
you, the receiver, are worthy

White roses
I wish to express spiritual love, purity, and innocence

Yellow roses
I, the giver, am jealous, or, more recently, I am sorry, or wish to express sympathy or ask for your remembrance

Dark pink roses
I am grateful or appreciative

Light pink
I admire you ⌛

FUNERAL PARLOR SECRETS

1 Shopping around for funeral services can save you thousands of dollars.
2 Funeral homes are businesses; funeral directors are businessmen, not clergy.
3 Seeing your loved one's body prior to embalming will not increase your grief, and public viewings without embalming are only illegal in Minnesota.
4 Embalming is usually unnecessary if burial is to take place between 24 and 48 hours after death; refrigeration is an alternative that some experts even say is preferable.
5 Sealed caskets do not preserve a body.
6 There is no need to spend more than $400–$600 on a casket.

NB While we're on the subject: There is no hard evidence to suggest that the preservatives in food are slowing the decomposition of corpses. ⌛

THE SING A SONG OF SIXPENCE CODE

Everyone thinks they know that the nursery rhyme "Ring a Ring o' Roses" refers to the plague, although this is actually a controversial issue. What is less known is that "Sing a Song of Sixpence" was probably a coded message sent by pirates on recruitment drives from the early 1700s onwards.

Piracy was illegal, so advertising had to be covert. "Sing a Song of Sixpence" is supposed to have been used by the men of the notorious Blackbeard. The first line told of a day rate of sixpence plus a leather bag full of whiskey. The second line told of the then common practice of hiding things in pies: Blackbeard's men (4 and 20 blackbirds) lying quietly in wait (baked in a pie) as those from the ship they intended to rob jumped aboard. When the "pie" was opened, the "birds" attacked with a mighty clamor; the ship was a "tasty dish" to set before the king of the pirates, Blackbeard.

Blackbeard was in his counting house counting out his crew's payments of sixpence. "The Queen"—his ship, *The Queen Anne's Revenge*—was in the port ("parlor") taking in supplies ("eating bread and honey"). "The maid" (a ship they were targeting for attack) was in "the garden" (an area above the Caribbean) "hanging out her clothes" (setting sail). When down came one of Blackbeard's pirates and "snapped off her nose." Which unfortunately remains obscure. ⌛

THE SECRET TO GETTING AN UPGRADE

Although a certain degree of luck is involved in getting an upgrade on commercial air flights—they only happen if economy is full—there are still ways of vastly improving your chances of having more legroom and better food.

First, consider signing up for an airline loyalty card. If you have managed to accrue sufficient air miles, the staff might upgrade you for free. Also, while standing in the check-in line, watch the staff and adopt your approach accordingly. If the staff member has been on the receiving end of a screaming match from an angry passenger, be super-sympathetic when it's your turn. Alternatively, become the person who complains—but do it nicely. If you have a genuine grievance, air your view and then ask, politely, about the possibility of an upgrade. And never give up. Keep asking at different locations—the check-in, the lounge, or the gate. Nothing is ever set in stone until you enter the plane. Still, certain features are sure-fire winners if you hope to turn left for free when you step on that plane. Research has proved that people with double-barreled surnames are far more likely to receive upgrades, as indeed are well-spoken men aged between 45 and 55. ❀

THE SECRET TO EATING RIGHT #1

Green tea protects your teeth and can help stop bad breath, as it kills bacteria found in the mouth and the flavoids contained within the leaves work with the active ingredients in toothpaste and mouthwash to boost their efficiency.

A strong cup of coffee before a workout can raise your heart rate and allow you to warm up quicker.

A high protein meal can increase your memory powers. Immediately. A protein burst will raise your levels of amino acids, which boost your short term memory for up to three hours.

A couple of drinks a day can help you stay sharp. Pan-European studies showed that those with a drinking-in-moderation culture such as France and Italy had better memories and sharper reactions, as small amounts of alcohol lowered LDL cholesterol, raising blood flow with no added strain in the heart, and therefore carrying more oxygen to the brain.

A WHISPERING GALLERY IN NEW YORK

St. Paul's Cathedral in London has a famous Whispering Gallery and New York has its own version at Grand Central Station. It is on the dining concourse, near the Oyster Bar, and takes the form of a vaulted tiled dome resting on four piers. The acoustics operate in such a way that a whisper from someone standing at one corner can be heard clearly by a listener standing diagonally across.

THE SECRET OF CREATIVITY

"THE SECRET TO CREATIVITY IS KNOWING HOW TO HIDE YOUR SOURCES."
Albert Einstein (*20th-century German physicist*)

"CREATIVITY COMES FROM TRUST. TRUST YOUR INSTINCTS. AND NEVER HOPE MORE THAN YOU WORK."
Rita Mae Brown (*20th-century American author*)

THE SECRETS OF IMPRESSING WOMEN

Neuro-linguistic programming (NLP) is a psychological tool discovered in the 1970s that uses language to communicate with the unconscious mind. It is the art of verbal persuasion, a kind of every-day hypnosis that can subtly alter a person's perception. NLP-related tricks have proved extremely successful in dating since the right kind of language can mean the two of you feel instantly connected. According to the principles of NLP, you should ask your lady friend a question and then match the language of her answer for the rest of the night. For example, ask her, "What do you find most fulfilling about your job?" This should elicit a response that includes such suggestive double-entendres as "passionate" and "stimulating."

Take note of the words she uses most frequently and keep repeating these favorite words of hers. She will feel an instant attraction—and have no idea why.

Or ask her to talk about a happy event from her past. While relaying this joyous anecdote she will subconsciously be transferring these fond memories onto you. Again, she will automatically feel connected to you.

A slightly more sinister NLP concept is using innocent phrases that sound like something else. "It's not below me to do that," for instance, could subconsciously be translated as "Blow me." Alternatively, bring into the conversation the subject of attractive men, maybe how you admire George Clooney for being the kind of man women adore and other men admire. While stating your opinions—beginning with "I think . . ." and so forth—emphatically pat your chest: the woman will instantly relate this talk of gorgeous George to you.

COLD WAR FALSE ALARM

At the North American Air Defense Command (NORAD) in 1979, a false alarm almost set off a catastrophic chain of events. A technician at the Cheyenne Mountain Complex in Colorado mistakenly inserted a training tape into the system. Astonished radar operators saw what appeared to be a huge Soviet missile attack on their screens. The early warning system set off the launch protocol for the U.S. nuclear response, but when no other tracking stations reported similar results, the fault was spotted. This and other less serious incidents prompted an overhaul of NORAD and its operations.

THE SECRET LIFE OF THOMAS EDISON

Everybody knows that Edison invented the light bulb and phonograph, and helped to invent the movies, but his life story also contains a chapter with a more sinister edge.

Not only was Edison an inventor, he was an entrepreneur who saw to it that he benefited financially from electricity at every stage and in every mode of its generation. In the early 1880s he profited from the light bulb, certainly, but also from New York City's use of cables, motors, and generators.

Then competition arrived in the form of George Westinghouse, who had developed the railroad air brake. His electricity system used alternating current (AC), which functioned over many miles, as opposed to Edison's direct current (DC), which could reach no more than a few hundred yards, meaning more noisy generators for cities.

Clearly Westinghouse was first in line to electrify the rest of the world. Edison's response was to capitalize on fears that AC currents were dangerous and begin a negative publicity campaign that backed up the notion, distributing pamphlets to cities that warned of the danger of his rival's system to families.

Meanwhile, Albany had been looking for a type of capital punishment less gory than hanging: botched hangings were leading to strangulation and even decapitation. A morphine injection was felt to be too pleasant a way to go; the guillotine too bloody. The Commission on Humane Executions asked Edison about using electrical currents.

At first he refused to help because he was opposed to capital punishment. Then, unable to resist what he saw as a marketing opportunity, he changed tack and returned to them recommending Westinghouse's alternating method. This, he believed, would inextricably link Westinghouse with death in the public's consciousness.

In fact, the tide had already turned against Westinghouse, beginning with unrest within his own company. In the event, Westinghouse's AC method was used for the first electrocution, but his condemnation of capital punishment came far too late. His cheap, efficient mode of electricity became preferred, but Edison's is the name we all remember. ⌛

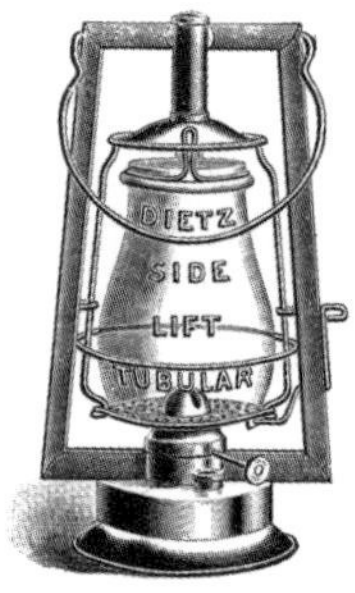

THE SECRET OF SUCCESSFUL PUBLIC SPEAKING

Speaking in public is one of the greatest fears of modern life. It doesn't come easily to most people, including politicians, which is why they employ crack squads of speech writers. Since most of us do not have the means to employ speech writers, we need to know the secrets of how to do it:

Relax. In order to avoid speaking with a squeaky voice, you will need to relax your body before you start. Shrug your shoulders, roll your neck, and make sure you are standing with an equal balance on both feet. Take a deep breath and then begin.
Keep it short. And, where appropriate, entertaining. Light-heartedness and brevity will ensure that the audience stays on your side.
Don't over prepare. And never write your speech out verbatim—reading from a script will make your speech sound dull. Instead, stick to two or three bullet points. Know your subject thoroughly and work around these points.
Consider your audience. Tailor your speech, jokes, and so forth to whomever you are addressing.
Make eye contact. Look at different people in the crowd, and don't focus on a single fixed point. If it makes you feel uncomfortable, look above your audience's heads rather than directly at their faces.
Speak slowly and clearly.
Change your tone. Emphasize key words—that way, any important points you have made will hopefully stick in the mind of your audience.
Consider adding a dramatic pause. This trick will alert the audience—and wake them up. So pause—and then punch.
Include your emotions. Scattering your speech with phrases such as "I feel" will endear you to your audience and make you appear more human.
Think in threes. The great Roman orator Cicero invented this device—the tripartite sentence—as a way of emphasizing his point. If you are including examples, for instance, always include them in threes, saving the most important one for last.
Control your hands. Don't hold them behind your back (it gives the impression that you're hiding something and distracts the audience) or clasp them in front, which can look too much like you are praying. Relax them by holding a pen in your free hand to avoid any awkwardness.
Control your feet. If you are moving around or rocking from side to side, the audience will be distracted from what you are saying. Instead, imagine your feet are set in concrete and you won't move an inch. ❀

ABANDONED LONDON TUBE STATIONS

There are around 40 abandoned stations on the London Underground. Some have disappeared completely, but the observant passenger may catch a sight of traces of others. The British Museum station was closed in the 1930s, but its white-tiled walls can be seen as Central Line trains pass between Tottenham Court Road and Holborn. During the war it was converted into an air raid shelter. The proposed Bull and Bush station on the Northern line between Hampstead and Golders Green, abandoned after opposition from local residents in 1906, was also enlisted into wartime service as a telecommunications point—today you can still see the outline of a staircase. In west London near the BBC Television Center, the old platforms and stairs of Wood Lane station can be seen from eastbound Central Line trains just after White City. In the east of the city at Whitechapel, traces of the old St. Mary's station can be glimpsed from the District Line. Some of the ghost stations have enjoyed an unusual afterlife. Aldwych station, on the Strand in central London, is regularly used for film and television shoots.

JOE DIMAGGIO AND THE CHURCH OF ST. PETER AND ST. PAUL

When Joe DiMaggio and Marilyn Monroe posed for wedding day snaps on the steps outside San Francisco's Church of St. Peter and St. Paul in January 1954, everyone assumed they'd married in the opulent church located at 666 Filbert Street. Nothing could be further from the truth: in fact, he'd married his first wife, show-girl Dorothy Arnold, in St. Peter and St. Paul in 1939, while he and Marilyn had wed in a quiet civil ceremony in San Francisco's City Hall nearby. DiMaggio also chose to be buried in St. Peter and St. Paul's cemetery after his death in 1999. Why the lifelong attachment to the church? As a kid growing up in San Francisco's North Beach area, he and his two baseball-playing brothers had attended the Salesian sports clubs run by Father Orestes Trinchieri of St. Peter and St. Paul's to keep poor boys off the streets. The sports training paid off and DiMaggio's astonishing baseball career began when he was picked up by the San Francisco Seals. He always remembered his early days and gave support to the church for helping him.

THE COW WHO DISCOVERED THE SECRET OF FIRE

On 8 October 1871, a fire broke out in a barn owned by Patrick and Catherine O'Leary. It spread rapidly through the largely wooden city and blazed for nearly two days. When it was over, hundreds were dead and much of the city was in ruins. The fire was begun, it is now thought, by a cow kicking over a lantern. The site of the barn where the cow lived is now the location of the training academy of the Chicago Fire Department, at the corner of Dekoven and Jefferson Streets.

SECRET US BIOLOGICAL WARFARE EXPERIMENTS

During the Cold War the U.S. military conducted secret germ warfare experiments on unwitting human subjects. In 1951, army scientists released supposedly harmless micro-organisms at the Norfolk Naval Supply Center in Virginia. Similar experiments on how bacteria might spread among the wider population were carried out at Washington National Airport in 1965. The traveling public were exposed to biological agents in a secret simulation of a germ warfare attack. In the 1970s it was revealed that bacteria and a variety of chemicals had been sprayed over the cities of St. Louis, San Francisco, and over another 200 populated areas since the 1950s. The army strongly denied that any of the micro-organisms could cause any harm, although mysterious illnesses and deaths have been linked to the experiments. On occasions, deadly substances have been used. In Utah in 1968, around 6,000 sheep were killed after the army released nerve gas 20 miles away.

THE FIRST THAMES TUNNEL

Now forgotten, the first Thames Tunnel was one of the great engineering achievements of 19th-century London. Designed by Marc Kingdom Brunel, the father of Isambard Kingdom Brunel, it ran under the river from Wapping to Rotherhithe. Begun in 1825 and opened to traffic nearly 20 years later, Brunel's tunnel was a revolutionary achievement, the first time that such an underwater tunneling project had succeeded. Over a million people passed through it in the four months after opening, although it struggled to make a financial return. By the 1860s it had acquired a reputation as a dangerous thoroughfare and haven for criminals. It was converted into a railway tunnel in 1869 and was eventually incorporated into the East London underground line. Today, visitors taking a ride on the East London line from Wapping to Rotherhithe travel through the tunnel.

HITLER'S HOROSCOPE

It is little known that Adolf Hitler—like Ronald Reagan after him—was interested in astrology. So much so in fact that during the Nazi rise to power in the '20s and '30s, he periodically consulted a Swiss astrologist called Karl Krafft. On the outbreak of war, British intelligence, who made it their business to know all of der Führer's secret passions, concocted a plan to use astrology to undermine Hitler's confidence. Since Hitler's birthday was on 20 April, his star sign was that of Taurus. As the date approached in 1941, British agents managed to plant a series of unfavorable horoscopes in newspapers around the world. In them it was suggested that Taureans would suffer reverses in the coming year and could come under threat from those closest to them. Which, of course, proved to be wholly correct. However, it is not known what affect these had on Hitler's state of mind or ability to make decisions.

HOLLYWOOD'S CRICKET SECRET

One of the movie capital's best-kept secrets was the Hollywood Cricket Club. During the mid-1930s, when Hollywood moguls were fascinated by anything and everything that came out of the British Empire, classic films such as *Charge of the Light Brigade*, *Lives of a Bengal Lancer*, *Clive of India*, and *Gunga Din* were all being filmed in Hollywood.

Consequently, large numbers of movie stars were plucked from the English stage and film studios, ferried across the Atlantic and dumped down in Tinseltown.

The Grand Old Man of the British expatriate community in Hollywood was undoubtedly C. Aubrey Smith. A larger-than-life character actor, Smith starred in a number of movies, among them *Rebecca*, *The Prisoner of Zenda*, and *Little Women*. In his off-screen moments, however, Sir Aubrey devoted himself to the Hollywood Cricket Club, and was never happier than when he was supervising the activities of the club, which opened in Los Angeles' Griffith Park in 1933.

Stars such as Laurence Olivier, Cary Grant, Ronald Colman, Boris Karloff, Errol Flynn, David Niven, and Basil Rathbone and Nigel Bruce (cinema's best-ever Sherlock Holmes and Watson) were all enthusiastic members of the Hollywood Cricket Club. Expatriate writers like James Hilton, Aldous Huxley, and P. G. Wodehouse were also an integral part.

The Hollywood Cricket Club is still in existence today.

HIDDEN DISASTER AT THE LUZHNIKI STADIUM

The former Soviet Union's ruling elite spent untold millions of roubles ensuring that the many tragic disasters that befell the U.S.S.R. were kept secret, hidden from the Western world. Formerly known as the Lenin Stadium, the Luzhniki now hosts the Moscow soccer teams Spartak and Torpedo. In 1982, however, it was the site of Europe's worst stadium disaster, when 340 Spartak fans were crushed to death at a European match against the Dutch team Haarlem. The incident was covered up by the Soviet authorities who said in the government newspaper *Izvestia* that only 66 people had been killed. The full death toll only emerged in 1989.

THE SECRET HISTORY OF IVORY SOAP

Procter and Gamble's Ivory Soap is said to have been so-named after Mr. Proctor had an epiphany when he heard the following quotation from Psalms in church: "All thy garments smell of myrrh and aloes and cassia, out of the ivory palaces whereby they have made thee glad." Which might be true and makes a good story anyway. The soap's most remarkable property, though, is that it floats. According to Proctor and Gamble folklore, this neat marketing trick came about by accident in the mid- to late-nineteenth century.

The story goes that in 1879, a hapless young employee who had been instructed to switch the soap mixing machine off at lunchtime forgot to do so, which resulted in more air being added to the soap than was normal, giving it a softer, fluffier texture. Hapless new boy told his supervisor about the blunder, goes the story, and they agreed to continue the production process as normal, packaging the soap and sending it out, hoping that no one would notice.

But before long, Proctor and Gamble were receiving letters saying how the soap was suddenly revolutionizing people's lives. Women were saying that the whole process of washing had been changed because the soap floated. The bosses sought the source of the change in its constituency and found hapless new boy and his accidental new technique. Both were retained, giving the soap its defining feature.

But there is recent evidence to suggest that this lovely story is just that—a story. Researchers hunting through company archives while in the process of compiling a book about the company found the diary of James N. Gamble, son of the Proctor and Gamble's co-founder. One 1863 entry reads: "I made floating soap today. I think we'll make all of our stock that way."

FLIGHT CONTROL SECRETS #1

Like French is the language of the professional kitchen, English is the language of the skies: everywhere in the world pilots and air traffic controllers communicate in English.

※ ※ ※

On flights, the pilots will be served the same meals as first class passengers, but they are not permitted to have the same dish for fear of food poisoning. For this reason they are not allowed to eat identical meals prepared in the same kitchen during the six hours before a flight.

※ ※ ※

It's common practice among cabin crew to take the odd blast of pure oxygen from the emergency cylinders to keep themselves sharp on long haul or overnight flights.

※ ※ ※

The amount of time cabin crew have off between shifts varies enormously from airline to airline as every country's aviation authority views it differently: American cabin crew have longer maximum shifts (19 hours) than British-based staff (16.5 hours) and a shorter minimum rest period (8 hours) as opposed to a full 24-hour day's rest if they have worked the maximum length.

※ ※ ※

It costs between $100,000 and $200,000 to train a pilot to commercial airline standards. Training can take up to 14 months, and that will be with previous flying experience—either in the Forces or light aircraft—as a background. Only 15 percent of all pilot applications received by British Airways are accepted for training.

THE SECRET OF LOVE

"LOVE CEASES TO BE A PLEASURE WHEN IT CEASES TO BE A SECRET."
Aphra Behn (*17th-century British playwright*)

HITLER'S SECRET FAMILY

A few last relatives of Adolf Hitler are still alive and reside in Long Island, New York, under false names.

Hitler's older brother Alois was touring through Britain—and studying the hotel industry—in 1909 when he met an Irish farm girl called Brigid in Dublin. They eloped to London and from there moved to Liverpool where, in 1911, they had a son named William Patrick.

Alois took over a small restaurant, a boarding house, and a hotel, but before very long he was bankrupt and returned to Germany, leaving his son, William Patrick, and Brigid, his wife. William Patrick's first attempt to obtain gainful employment, at a company called Benhan & Son, Ltd., in London in the 1930s was thwarted when his potential employer learned of his surname. His response was to go to Germany to see if he could capitalize on his surname there. His father and uncle, the Führer, duly found him work as a bookkeeper, but William Patrick felt he deserved better things. So he approached his uncle making it clear that he wanted a more prestigious position and threatening, by some accounts, to reveal that Adolf Hitler's grandfather was an Austrian Jew if he did not see to it that his position was elevated.

Hitler ordered William Patrick—"my loathsome nephew"—to renounce his British citizenship and take a senior position in the Third Reich. Instead, he fled. It was 1939, however, and he was not welcome in London. Still determined to make that name a help rather than a hindrance, he signed up with the William Morris Theatrical Agency and at their instigation headed for the U.S. with his mother on the French liner *Normandie*. He went on a lecture tour, giving talks on the subject of his Uncle Adolf.

At first there was a degree of public interest in his lectures, but by the time America had joined the war in 1941, this was drying up. It was then that he decided to go to the top again. On 3 March, 1942 he composed a letter to President Roosevelt. "I am the nephew and only descendent of the ill famed Chancellor and Leader of Germany," he wrote, "who today so despotically seeks to enslave the free and Christian peoples of the globe. I am respectfully submitting this petition to you to enquire as to whether I may be allowed to join [the U.S. army] in their struggle against tyranny and oppression." He went on, adding that "The British are an insular people and while they are kind and courteous, it is my impression, rightly or wrongly, that they could not in the long run feel overly cordial or sympathetic to an individual bearing the name I do."

J. Edgar Hoover ordered the FBI to

conduct an investigation into William Patrick's "background, activities, associates and loyalties" and suggested "that he be discreetly thoroughly interviewed for pertinent data." "Confidential Informer No.2," a man who had been lined up to ghost a book that William Patrick had been planning, described him as using "mild blackmail" on Adolf Hitler to get work in Germany, using the fact that Alois had remarried without obtaining a divorce from his first wife, William Patrick's mother.

Although "Confidential Informer No.1" agreed with William Patrick's story that he left Germany and his uncle due to the regime there, "Confidential Informer No.2" seemed to think it was more to do with the fact that his uncle was only prepared to help him get a job that matched his qualifications. He went further, pulling no punches: "Informant 2 said that subject Hitler was an exceedingly lazy individual, had no initiative and constantly sought a position which paid well with little work. In his opinion if Adolf Hitler had secured for the subject an important position which paid well, the subject would have been an ardent Nazi and a supporter of Adolf Hitler."

William Patrick was rejected by army officials when they read the part of the alien questionnaire that asked whether the applicant has or has had any relative serving in other armies. William had written: 1, Thomas J. Dowling, uncle, England, 1923–1926 Royal Air Force. 2, Adolf Hitler, uncle, Germany, 1914–1918, Corporal.

But the FBI investigation did not suggest that William Patrick was engaged in subversive activities of any kind, so in 1944 he was permitted to join the U.S. Navy. Part way through his service he was wounded in action, at which point he retreated to the countryside where he set up a blood analysis laboratory.

In Germany in the 1930s he had met a woman named Phyllis, the sister of a friend, and they had fallen in love. In 1947 the couple married and went on to have three sons who are alive and well and living anonymously in the U.S.

William Patrick died in 1987 at the age of 76 and was buried under a false name. Curiously, none of his three sons married or have any children. There is intriguing speculation that a pact may have been made between them to discontinue the bloodline. The oldest son, a social worker, is said to have at first denied this and then stated that he at least had not made a pact, although his brothers, who run a gardening business together, might have.

William Patrick, his oldest son, and "Informer No.1" were all adamant that he was no Nazi sympathizer or supporter of Hitler. Yet, when it came to giving his first born a middle name, and he had the pick of all the names in the world, why did he choose Adolf? ⌛

THE SECRET OF BEING A GOOD BOSS

You may have been taught to perform a multitude of job-related skills to perfection, but few of us are ever taught the secret of how to be a good boss. Here's the secret of how to achieve that.

To really succeed as a boss, you need to become a psychopath. Yes, *really*. According to recent research by a British university, the vast majority of office managers have personality traits that are almost identical with criminal psychopaths—in other words, psychiatric patients and hospitalized criminals—only altered by the fact they are law-abiding and marginally less impulsive. These traits include: the ability to be emotionally detached, egocentric, a mindless perfectionist, an expert in turning on the superficial charm, and willing to use and discard other people at whim. Lying, cheating, and general ruthlessness will get you to the top and help to keep you there.

However, if you're not psychopath material, consider the following:

Set a good example for your staff to live up to. Your office moral code should include never taking credit for something another employee has done, being scrupulously honest, and sharing as much company news as feasibly possible with your staff. Do this and you show respect for your workforce, something that will instill company loyalty.

Trust each employee to do their own work to the best of their ability. Define their duties clearly and regularly ask their opinions. Then give continuous feedback and praise good work.

Praise in public; criticize in private.

Really get to know your team—not only their positions but also their home life. If you are starting in a new office, make sure you have a one-on-one meeting with each member of the staff to find out what they hope to achieve and where their ambitions lie.

Fight for what your staff want—if it's a raise, make sure they realize you are doing everything in your power to make it happen.

You should also delegate wisely—you will *always* achieve more as a team than on your own.

Become a mentor to juniors, show a caring side of your personality that won't be forgotten. In business, what goes around comes around, and today's bright intern could be tomorrow's CEO. ❀

ABANDONED NEW YORK SUBWAY STATIONS #7

JEROME AVENUE

LOCATION: JEROME STREET AT 162 STREET

OPENED JULY 1918, CLOSED AUGUST 1958.

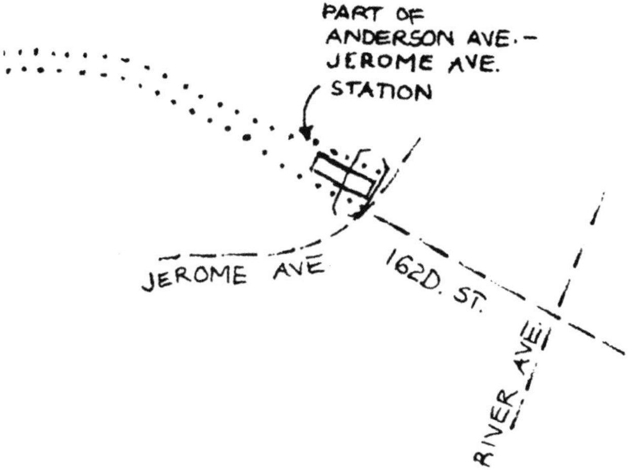

The station shares a history with the Sedgwick Avenue station. Situated at the end of a short tunnel used to connect the 6 Avenue and 9 Avenue elevated line at 155 St. in Manhattan to the newer elevated line in Jerome Avenue (which runs over River Avenue near 162 St), Jerome Avenue station emerged from a cliff face. Most of it was on a concrete-clad viaduct over Jerome Ave, the type of structure called an "ornamental el" that was built over parkways. West of the viaduct, the station extends over a building and then continues a short way into the tunnel. A portion in the tunnel and over the building remains.

THE TOP 20 SECRETS OF MAKING FRIENDS AND INFLUENCING PEOPLE

How To Win Friends And Influence People was the title of Dale Carnegie's groundbreaking 1937 book, probably the most famous self-help book of all time—it has now sold over 15 million copies. However, the world has somewhat changed since then and so the following advice should prove much more useful in the modern world.

ONE

Make people feel as important and appreciated as they believe they really are.

TWO

Become a good listener. Everyone loves talking about themselves.

THREE

Do not argue. Ever. In an argument, no one ever comes out the winner.

FOUR

If you find yourself the bearer of bad news, think of a way to soften the blow, maybe with a gift.

FIVE

When handling people, never criticize or complain. If you have a criticism to make, start with some praise and appreciation of their performance. Or talk about your own shortcomings before mentioning someone else's.

SIX

Find out—and remember—the names of your boss's kids or their favorite hobbies. He or she will start believing that you fit perfectly into the company, thus making promotion a more likely prospect for you than for a rival colleague who shows no interest.

SEVEN

To make someone do what you want, make them think that it was their idea in the first place.

EIGHT

If you are wrong, admit it instantly and emphatically.

NINE

Make "less is more" your personal mantra. In a business situation, say little and let other people do most of the talking. The same goes for emails—if you keep them short there is less scope for misinterpretation.

TEN

Create a mystique about yourself. If you are ever-so-slightly enigmatic and sphinx-like, people are less likely to put you in a box.

ELEVEN

In any situation, try and see it from the other person's point of view.

TWELVE

Ask questions and don't give direct orders.

THIRTEEN

Be encouraging. Praise every improvement.

FOURTEEN

Give people an excellent reputation to live up to.

FIFTEEN

When you are tempted to react to something, ignore your initial feeling and let it go. Knee-jerk reactions do not bode well in business.

SIXTEEN

Make sure that people are dependent on you.

SEVENTEEN

Remember that your reputation is priceless and crucial if you want power. As Warren Buffett, the legendary investor, once said, "It takes 20 years to build a reputation and 5 minutes to ruin it." So never put your name on something you are less than 100 percent proud of.

EIGHTEEN

Work as a team and never become too isolated. Success rarely goes to the outsider; influence never does. You will always need your allies.

NINETEEN

Don't be too perfect. A few well-chosen flaws will make you appear more human. And never perform any task better than your boss—he or she will always want to feel superior and unthreatened.

TWENTY

Remember that it's lonely at the top.

THE SECRET HISTORY OF OLIVER CROMWELL'S HEAD

Oliver Cromwell, who ruled the short-lived English republic as Lord Protector, died in 1658. A deeply divisive figure, he was not allowed to rest in peace. After the restoration of the monarchy in 1660, Parliament set about meting out symbolic justice to those who had sent King Charles I to the scaffold. In 1661, Cromwell's remains were exhumed, hanged at Tyburn, decapitated, then his head was displayed on a spike at Westminster Hall for over a hundred years. Its whereabouts are then unrecorded until it was sold to one Josiah Wilkinson in 1815. He carried out tests on the skull to establish its authenticity, and kept it in the family as an heirloom. In 1960, Cromwell's skull was buried at a hidden location in Sidney Sussex College in Cambridge, where he had been a student.

THE SECRETS OF INSECT SURVIVAL

Everyone knows that the stick insect pretends to be a stick, but there is also a caterpillar that masquerades as a twig. Grey and knobbly in a twig-like kind of way, it freezes into position when it senses a predator, pretending to be an unappetizing piece of wood. The Walkingstick is another insect imposter. Long, thin, and brown with knobbly bits at both ends, it plays dead during the day, not moving an insect muscle—which is no mean feat, as any artist's model knows—but comes to life at night when it is on the lookout for tasty leaves. Hopefully the Katydid doesn't share the same neighborhood or its own form of disguise could be its downfall. Scuttling around the forest floor at night, it looks just like a leaf blown about by the wind, its large wings resembling leaves complete with fine veins.

JIMI HENDRIX AND JAYNE MANSFIELD'S SECRET DATE

Jimi Hendrix is regularly voted the greatest rock guitarist who ever played. His peerless reputation is based on such classic psychedelic singles as "Purple Haze," "The Wind Cries Mary," and "Voodoo Chile" as well as groundbreaking albums like *Electric Ladyland*. But before he broke through in the Swinging London of 1967, the Seattle-born guitarist had taken part in hundreds of sessions as an anonymous gun-for-hire. And of all those mid-60s sessions with the likes of Little Richard and the Isley Brothers, the most bizarre was surely the occasion when Hendrix found himself playing on the 1967 single "As The Clouds Drift By," sung by non-other than the poor man's Marilyn Monroe, Jayne Mansfield.

Mansfield died later that year, decapitated in a car crash aged just 34. And although she was not best remembered for her musical credentials, being backed by rock's greatest guitarist was not her only claim to pop fame—Mansfield also appeared in what many still regard as the greatest ever rock & roll movie, 1956's *The Girl Can't Help It*.

THE INDEX OF PROHIBITED BOOKS

During the 16th-century Counter-Reformation, the Catholic Church took action to defend its faith from theological contamination and immorality. The first Index *Librorum Prohibitorum* (Index of Prohibited Books) was drawn up in 1559 under the direction of Pope Paul IV, in response to the challenge of Protestantism. The Index was always controversial and liberal voices within the Church questioned its right to act as censor. However, it survived with regular reissues for over 400 years until it was suppressed in 1966. Which is not to say that there is no longer a list of books deemed unsuitable for devout Catholics to own or read. Indeed, books that are proclaimed as containing heretical views or views antithetical to the Roman Catholic Church are denied a Catholic audience by order of the Holy Father.

Works that appeared in the Index included those by the philosophers Descartes, Nicolaus Copernicus, Hume, Kant, and Sartre, and novelists such as Stendhal, Hugo, Richardson, Flaubert, Daniel Defoe, and Honoré Balzac, as well as the Dutch sexologist Theodor Hendrik van de Velde, author of the sex manual *The Perfect Marriage*. There have also been political magazines and periodicals included on the Index. Although the Index is no longer published, the Church still issues *"admonitums"* against works that might threaten to corrupt faith or morals.

CODEBREAKING AT BLETCHLEY PARK

In the secret history of the Second World War, the codebreaking operation at Bletchley Park is a remarkable chapter. At the outbreak of war, intelligence personnel began arriving at Bletchley Park, 50 miles north-west of London. Known as Station X, it would be home to an exceptional group of cryptologists and code breakers, whose efforts were a vital contribution to allied victory. German military communications were encrypted using the Enigma cipher machine. This was a complex electro-mechanical device that used a series of rotating "wheels" to scramble texts into ciphers. It was thought to be unbreakable, as there were a staggering 150 million million million different combinations, each one of which could produce a different coded message. However, in the 1930s, the Poles, led by mathematician Marian Rejewski, made significant inroads into Enigma, and constructed a machine similar to that used by the Germans. As the German invasion of Poland approached, the cipher was changed on a daily basis and the Poles effectively lost the ability to monitor German messages. So they turned over what they knew to the British and French, accelerating the progress at Bletchley Park.

The first success was founded upon the one apparent flaw in the Enigma code; a letter could not be encrypted as itself. In other words, a "T" would never appear in a coded message as a "T." From the early 1940s, a motley assortment of linguists, chess champions, and crossword addicts began to crack Enigma. The British mathematician Alan Turing speeded up the process by designing the Bombe, a machine that could rapidly process so-called "cribs," combinations of letters that appeared regularly in German messages, and were assumed to be proper names or common phrases. The Bombe would process each of these cribs and would gradually eliminate potential Engima settings until the correct one remained.

Other successes at Bletchley included breaking the Lorenz code, a cipher created by a machine even more complex than Enigma and used by the German high command. To do this, the British developed the Colossus, a programmable, electronic, information-processing machine and a forerunner of modern computers.

The intelligence coming out of Bletchley Park was codenamed Ultra, a reflection of how highly prized the secrets were. The success of the secret cipher breakers of Bletchley Park influenced the outcome of the Battle of Britain, the campaign against U-boats in the Atlantic, the North African campaign, the D-Day landings and, ultimately, the outcome of the war itself.

LITTLE KNOWN CULINARY CURIOS #4

Use a large paper clip to remove the stones from fresh cherries—push it in to the top, hook it around the stone, and pull!

To keep red cabbage's color during cooking, add lemon juice or vinegar to the water.

When making apple sauce, use large pieces that will cook quicker—water heats up inside them and blows them apart.

Open a can of asparagus at the bottom, so that the spears can be pulled out without damaging the tips.

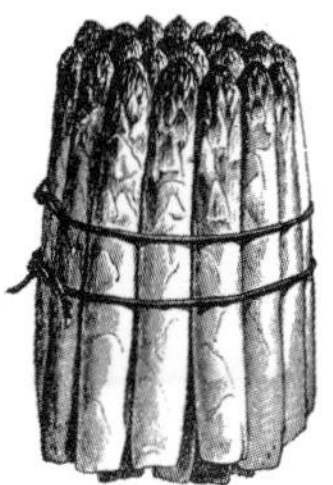

Bigger, darker, more open-cupped mushrooms have more flavor than small white button mushrooms.

To peel a tomato, make a small cross cut at the base, remove the eye (where it joined the vine), then immerse it in boiling water for 10 seconds. The skin should slide off, but the tomato won't have started cooking.

To soften butter, bang it on a hard surface. Kinetic energy heats up the molecules and softens the block.

Baked potatoes can be cooked on a bed of salt deep enough to reach about a third of the way up their sides.

When preparing salad, break or tear lettuce leaves instead of cutting them—the impact of the knife can bruise leaves and turn the cut edge brown.

FAMOUS AMERICAN FREEMASONS

BENJAMIN FRANKLIN
U.S. inventor of the lightning rod, 1746

GEORGE WASHINGTON
U.S. president between 1789 and 1797

THEODORE ROOSEVELT
U.S. president between 1901 and 1909

HENRY FORD
U.S. car manufacturer, created the Model T Ford in 1908

J. EDGAR HOOVER
Head of the FBI between 1924 and 1972

SIMON BOLIVAR
South American freedom fighter, Bolivia named in his honor in 1825

CHARLES LINDBERGH
U.S. aviator, made the first solo transatlantic flight, 1927

FRANKLIN D. ROOSEVELT
U.S. president between 1933 and 1945

HARLAND SANDER
AKA Col. Sanders, U.S. founder of KFC, created his secret recipe in 1939

GEORGE C. MARSHALL
U.S. general, chief of staff 1939 until 1945; winner Nobel Peace Prize 1953

DOUGLAS MACARTHUR
U.S. Army general, commander of Allied Forces in the Pacific WWII, 1941–45

IRVING BERLIN
U.S. songwriter, author of White Christmas, 1942

HARRY S. TRUMAN
U.S. president between 1945 and 1953

ROY ROGERS
U.S. actor and professional cowboy, star of his eponymous TV show, 1951–1964

ERNEST BORGNINE
U.S. actor, Academy Award winner in 1955 for best Actor in *Marty*

EDWIN "BUZZ" ALDRIN
Astronaut, second man to walk on the moon, 1969

GERALD FORD
U.S. president between 1974 and 1977.

THE SECRET OF SUCCESSFUL FLIRTING

Marilyn Monroe, Henry Kissinger, and Bill Clinton were all world-class experts in the art of flirting. Successful flirts aren't necessarily born, however, they can be made, which is why flirting academies are cropping up in many metropolitan cities. Here are some top flirting secrets:

WORK ON YOUR ENTRANCE INTO A ROOM.
Pause when you enter the room, survey the scene, put your shoulders back, and then continue walking.

DON'T BE PART OF A CROWD.
It can appear intimidating. Stand slightly apart from the rest to signify your individuality.

MAXIMIZE YOUR DIRECT EYE CONTACT.
Hold it for a little longer than is normal, and then immediately lower your eyes.

REPEAT A PERSON'S NAME.
This will instantly make them feel special.

CREATE AND USE A NICKNAME.
The two of you will form an instant, exclusive bond.

MIRROR THE OTHER PERSON'S BODY LANGUAGE.
The most revealing body language happens below the waist, so point your feet toward the object of your flirting.

WEAR OR CARRY SOMETHING UNUSUAL.
It can be a handy talking point.

BE UPBEAT.
Don't dwell on any problems or personal troubles.

REVEAL YOUR INNER WRIST.
It makes you appear vulnerable and ripe for seduction.

ASK "SOULFUL" QUESTIONS
Such as "Do you believe in love at first sight?" or "Do you love someone because you need them, or need them because you love them?"

AIM FOR AN ACCIDENTAL TOUCH.
For instance, reach for the door handle at the same time. Sparks will fly.

SUBTLY RUB YOUR THIGH IN A RHYTHMICAL AND REPETITIVE MANNER.
It will subconsciously draw the attention of the person you're talking to toward the groin area. ❀

COLD WAR SECRET: THE WOODPECKER SIGNAL

In 1976 a mysterious powerful shortwave radio signal began to create havoc with broadcasters and amateur users of the bands across the world. It was nicknamed the "Woodpecker," because the interference it caused sounded like the bird's incessant pecking. NATO direction-finders eventually traced the source of the signal to an area around Gomel in the U.S.S.R.. What was it? Most thought it was connected to an experimental over-the-horizon radar system, designed to detect enemy aircraft and missiles. Psychic warfare experts had a different theory, however. These radio waves, they claim, can be used to affect the moods or behavior of entire populations.

LITTLE KNOWN CULINARY CURIOS #4

Be careful not to eat pineapple skin. It contains a natural chemical that will irritate the inside of the mouth.

Never add salt or pepper to a reduction until it is reduced, otherwise the amount of seasoning will be disproportionate to the diminished liquid.

When boiling sprouts, cabbage, or broccoli, a piece of stale bread in the water will greatly reduce cooking odors. However, it is much better for taste and health to steam these vegetables.

If you are making your own bread crumbs, either use stale bread or slice it and put it in a warm oven to dry out; if it is still soft it will squash instead of disintegrating into crumbs.

Bananas will go black if you keep them in the fridge, but they will still be all right inside.

THE SECRET SOUTH AFRICAN COMMUNITY OF GAMKASKLOOF

Nestled between the mountains of the Swartberg range between Oudtshoorn and Prince Albert in South Africa's Western Cape lies an isolated, fertile valley. Legend has it that the Gamkaskloof community was started there when a solitary herdsman discovered the valley while looking for his cattle. By 1830, several families had traveled there either on foot or horseback, and settled. They must have shared a pioneering spirit and a lot of determination, because getting to the valley involved either crossing a river gorge or a steep mountain range.

For 130 years this community of over 100 people subsisted and thrived. Milk was produced by goats, pigs provided meat, fish came from the river, and honey could be obtained from the mountains. Donkeys were prized possessions and used for transport and to pull ploughs. Every few months a farmer would load up a train of donkeys with Gamkaskloof produce and go to the nearest town—several days' walk away—and trade dried figs, raisins, and animal skins for coffee, sugar, fabrics, and tools with which to work the land.

At the end of the 1950s, a group of men carried the community's first car into the valley, and four years later a gravel road was built. By 1965 telephones were installed in Gamkaskloof. It was no longer an isolated community. Other factors combined to end the era: drought, and information for the younger generation about an outside world full of possibilities. By the 1980s many farms had been sold and a decade on, the majority of the valley became the Swartberg Nature Reserve.

In 1999, restoration began on the traditional raw clay brick houses that had been left to the elements. Now they provide self-catering accommodation for visitors who come to the Nature Reserve to witness the beauty of the landscape and its plants and animals.

THE SIMPLE SECRET OF LIVING LONGER

A 15-year Greek study that concluded in the early 21st century contrasted the cardiovascular health and death rates of men and women living in lowland and upland villages, 3,300 feet above sea level. Although their lives were similar in all other respects, the mountain dwellers lived longer and had less heart disease than the plains dwellers. The answer to longer life, researchers concluded, is to move to the mountains. Living in the less oxygen-rich air at moderate altitude causes physiological changes that strengthen heart function.

HITLER'S GASSED COUSIN

When the Nazis gassed to death those unfortunate thousands with mental illnesses, one of the victims was Hitler's second cousin.

Aloisia V, who according to her medical files suffered problems that included schizophrenia, depression, and delusions, was the great granddaughter of the sister of Hitler's paternal grandmother and was gassed at a mental institution in Austria on 6 December 1940, aged 49.

In a secret 1944 report, the Nazis had labeled her line of the family, the Schicklgrubers, "idiotic progeny." U.S. historians Florian Beierl and Timothy Ryback established that several of the Schicklgrubers suffered from mental illness and had even committed suicide, and that eventually the line died out. No one knows whether Hitler was aware of the fate of his cousin, nor yet whether he suffered from mental illness himself. ⌛

SECRET EXPLOSIONS #2

When zeppelin airships were employed on bombing runs by the German military in World War I, they flew so low that planes could fly over them and drop bombs on them.

※ ※ ※

In 1605, after Guy Fawkes's plotters had laid the barrels of gunpowder in the tunnels under the Houses of Parliament in London, they gathered on what would be called Parliament Hill, about 4 miles north of Westminster, to watch the blast. It never came, as their plan had been discovered and they were soon to be arrested.

※ ※ ※

At 63,032 degrees Fahrenheit, the explosion caused by a lightning flash is five times hotter than the surface of the sun.

※ ※ ※

You can hear explosions under water because water conducts sound waves.

APHRODITE'S SECRET ARMY

The ancient Goddess of Love, Aphrodite was worshipped by everyone in ancient Babylon (modern-day Iraq). So important was she considered that prostitution was sacred and institutionalized among the babylonians, and all women were expected at least once in their lives to have sex with a stranger who paid for it.

Writing in around 450 B.C., Herodotus told how in the Babylonian temples of Aphrodite, women sat waiting until a man threw a silver coin into their lap. In order to do her sacred duty to the goddess of love, a woman was obliged to have sex in the temple grounds with the first man who paid before she could go home.

GONE WITH THE WIND SECRETS

How different it could all have been: imagine Lucille Ball as Pansy O'Hara in *Baa Baa Black Sheep* . . . or Bette Davis as Angel O'Hara in *Not In Our Stars* . . . or even Mae West as Storm O'Hara in *Tote the Weary Load*. . . . These are just some of the strange ways in which *Gone With the Wind*, the film seen by more people on the planet than any other, could have turned out.

At one time or another, Bette Davis, Lana Turner, Paulette Goddard, Susan Hayward, Katherine Hepburn, and Mae West were all shortlisted for Scarlett O'Hara, the most coveted role in film history. And when the nationwide search came to Atlanta, over 500 Southern belles turned up, including every Miss Atlanta since 1917!

In 1939, after three years and more than $4 million spent trying to bring *Gone With the Wind* to the screen, producer David O. Selznick's troubles still weren't over. Author Margaret Mitchell had written Rhett Butler's farewell to Scarlett as "My dear, I don't give a damn." But somewhere along the line "frankly" was added, giving the line greater emphasis and the movie its infamous adieu. In an attempt to minimize offence and mollify the censors, Clark Gable put the stress on "give" rather than the final swear word. But the censors of the time were not fooled, and fined Selznick $5,000 for including the profanity.

THE SECRETS OF MANIPULATION TECHNIQUES USED BY PRODUCT MANUFACTURERS

We are very obedient when it comes to following instructions on the products we buy, and the manufacturers know it. Famously, back in the 1930s, Lever brothers asked their employees for suggestions on how to improve their shampoo sales. One bright spark suggested the addition of the word "Repeat" to the directions written on bottles. Voila—sales were doubled.

In the 1960s, Alka Seltzer began a marketing campaign to remove its associations with the elderly and with overindulgent slobs who ate and/or drank too much. They did so using humor, but more crucially, although the directions on the packet said it was only necessary to use one tablet, the advertisements featured two tablets clunking and fizzing into a glass of water with a "plop plop, fizz fizz" catchline. The effect on sales was immediately positive.

Consider too the arrival of the tiny words "After opening, refrigerate" and sometimes "Eat within 8 weeks" on sauce bottles. They weren't there when the product was first sold. The benefit to the manufacturer of the latter is obvious: if you obey, you will get through or dispose of the bottle more quickly and replace it with another. The former, however, is brilliant. If you store your bottle in the refrigerator, probably in the door, you will be reminded of it every time you open it. Stuck in a cupboard you will forget it is there and will use it less often. They know us better than we know ourselves. ⌛

THE SECRET SEARCH FOR THE GOD PARTICLE

There's a secret underground race on to prove the existence of the so-called "God particle" that physicists theorize gives matter its mass, and explains how the universe was made. 330 feet below the city suburbs of Geneva is a 17-mile tunnel which houses the newly built Large Hadron Collider, the brainchild of particle physicists at Cern, the European-funded Laboratory for Particle Physics.

Near Chicago in the United States is the underground 7-mile Fermilab Tevatron particle accelerator. In these tunnels, high-energy beams of protons and antiprotons will be accelerated around in both directions, so the particles collide. It's hoped the results will show that the God particle or Higg's boson (named after the British physicist Peter Higgs who suggested its existence in the late 1960s), really does exist.

THE SECRET OF DINING IN THE DARK

The strangest restaurant in Paris is Dans le Noir (In the Dark), where diners eat in total darkness. The waiters are all blind and for a short time their customers experience something similar. The menu can be studied beforehand, although you can opt for a surprise menu. Diners speak of a dislocation of the senses, as the connection between sight and taste is broken. The restaurant is located at 51 Rue Quincampoix.

PAUL McCARTNEY'S SONGWRITING SECRETS

Late in 1963, Paul McCartney woke up one morning in his bedroom at 57 Wimpole Street, London, with a melody running through his head. He couldn't write music, and this was in the days before successful home recording equipment, so the Beatle immediately ran through the melody on the piano he kept beside his bed. Over the next couple of months he would play the song to anyone he met: fellow Beatles, producer George Martin, director Dick Lester, singer Alma Cogan . . . because McCartney was convinced that the melody he had dreamed was not original.

He thought it must be something he had subconsciously remembered from a television ad, or from a tune his father Jim had played back in Liverpool. Meanwhile, to keep the melody fresh in his mind, the 21-year-old McCartney added a swiftly improvised lyric: "Scrambled eggs, ooh baby, how I love your legs."

Everyone he played it to was convinced the tune was an original. And eventually, in May 1965, while on holiday in Portugal, McCartney realized that the little melody he had literally dreamed up needed some slightly more promising lyrics. Which is when "Scrambled Eggs" metamorphosed into "Yesterday"—which in turn became the most popular song in the history of recorded music.

"Yesterday" was only one of three tracks The Beatles recorded on 14 June 1965. That same afternoon they also cut the roaring "I'm Down" and Paul's boisterous "I've Just Seen a Face," and the first the outside world knew of the song was when it appeared on The Beatles's fifth album *Help!* In America the single version of "Yesterday" remained at #1 for a month during 1965, but, strangely, it was not released as a single in the UK until 1976, when it reached #8.

By 2005 there had been an estimated 3,000 cover versions.

ABANDONED NEW YORK SUBWAY STATIONS #8

91 STREET

LOCATION: 91 AT BROADWAY

OPENED OCTOBER 1904, CLOSED AUGUST 1959.

A shallow station like 18 Street and Worth Street, 91 shares a similar early history. Originally built to avoid a ten block stretch without a station, it was closed in 1959 when 96 Street was extended to 94 Street.

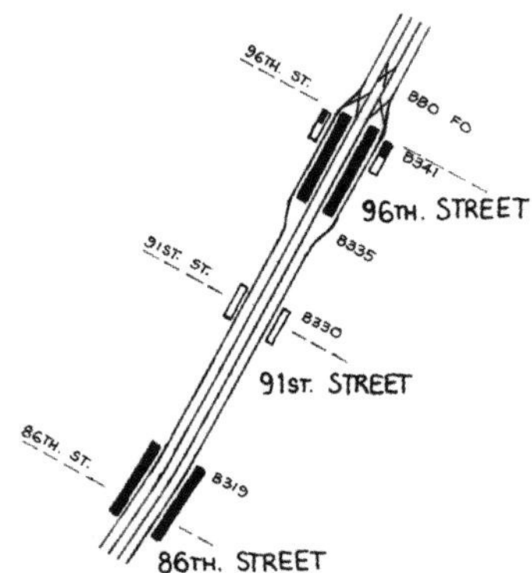

THE BRITISH SCHINDLER

In 2004 a plaque was unveiled at the British Embassy in Berlin honoring a man described as a British Schindler. Passport Officer and MI6 spy Frank Foley helped thousands of Berlin's Jews escape Germany in the 1930s by providing them with visas to Britain and the territories it controlled. Most of this was done in contravention of the orders of the British Foreign Office, which was trying to limit Jewish immigration in all but exceptional cases. Foley accelerated his efforts on behalf of German Jews in the period before the war as the Nazi persecution intensified. By the time he left Berlin at the outbreak of war, he had saved an estimated 10,000 people. He later interrogated Rudolph Hess after the Nazi had gone to Scotland, but his earlier efforts on behalf of Berlin's Jews went unrecognized in his home country. In 1999, he was honored by Israel with the status of a "Righteous Among the Nations" in recognition of his conduct.

THE SECRET TO FINDING A HUSBAND

Adopt the following advice if you want to marry Mr. Right.

MOVE TO THE COUNTRYSIDE.
Research proves that statistically there are more single women in cities and, conversely, more single men in rural areas.

GET OUT MORE.
Find eligible men in the gym, in coffee shops, on the train, or join an evening class with a guaranteed high quota of the opposite sex (think military history). Be friendly and make an effort to strike up conversations.

MAKE THE FIRST MOVE.
Men are more confused than ever about when it is considered appropriate to pounce. Erase any confusion for him.

DO NOT APPROACH A MAN WHO IS OVER THE AGE OF 40.
Again, research shows that the likelihood of a man marrying post-40 (with the exception of divorcés) reduces drastically. These men are confirmed bachelors and set in their unattached ways.

BE SUPER-CONFIDENT ABOUT EVERYTHING FROM THE WAY YOU CARRY YOURSELF TO YOUR OPINIONS.
Confidence is like catnip.

TAKE CARE OF YOUR APPEARANCE.
Make the most of what you have and accentuate the positive. Also, always expose a small amount of flesh—perhaps an ankle, your wrists or the nape of your neck—as this subconsciously reveals your warm inner nature.

BECOME A GREAT LISTENER.
Men love talking about themselves and will feel instantly comfortable in front of a willing audience.

TREAT YOUR SINGLE STATUS AS A BUSINESS PLAN.
Announce to everyone you know that you are on the look-out for single men—friends of friends often make the best dates as they have already been vetted. Devote a third of your earnings to self-improvement including expensive haircuts, a new wardrobe, gym membership, etc.

BECOME A PRAYING MANTIS AND DON'T BE AFRAID TO CHASE.
Many men eventually submit to highly motivated man-eaters. You can easily convince a man he can't survive without you—if only because he hasn't been given the chance. ❀

THE SECRET OF BARGAIN HUNTING (ELECTRICAL GOODS)

OFFER TO PAY IN CASH.
Even the electrical departments in the most glitzy of department stores may do a deal if you're not using a credit card.

PLAY DUMB.
And act friendy. Ask for the salesman's advice. He will be flattered that you are putting your trust in him and will thus be much more likely to offer you a great deal.

ASK FOR EXTRAS.
If you feel like haggling, simply ask: "What's the best price you can do this for?" If the salesman is unwilling to offer a discount, ask about free delivery or installation.

GO TO THE LAST DAY OF A TRADE EXHIBITION.
Since the exhibitors will be packing up their stands, they might sell their goods off cheap instead of carrying them home. ❀

LITTLE KNOWN CULINARY CURIOS #5

The smoother an orange's skin, the thinner it will be, therefore that fruit will yield more juice. You can also judge an orange's relative juice content by its weight—the heavier it is the more juice you will get from it.

Rinse the pan out with water before boiling milk in it—that will make it much easier to clean afterwards as the milk will not stick to the sides.

When frying bacon, stop it curling up by making a few quarter-inch cuts in the fatty edge.

The best crème fraiche comes from Normandy in northern France.

If jams or jellies are having difficulty setting, add sliced apples, as the fruit is rich in pectin, nature's setting agent.

THE SECRETS OF GIVING FLOWERS #3

Common flowers and their secret meanings according to Victorians:

Acacia (rose or white): *elegance, friendship*
Acacia (yellow): *secret love*
Aloe: *grief, misplaced devotion, superstition*
Ambrosia: *love reciprocated*
Anemone: *fading hope, unfading love*
Ash: *prudence, you are safe with me*
Azalea: *moderation, temperance*
Begonia: *beware*
Bluebell: *humility, constancy*
Camellia (red): *genuine excellence, warmth*
Camellia (white): *perfect loveliness*
Carnation: *fidelity, fascination*
Carnation (pink): *I will not forget you*
Carnation (yellow): *you have disappointed me, rejection*
Cherry blossom: *spiritual beauty*
Chestnut blossom: *do me justice*
Chrysanthemum (red): *I love*
Chrysanthemum (white): *truth, innocence*
Clematis: *mental beauty*
Daffodil: *deceit, hope, unrequited love*
Dahlia: *elegance, dignity, I am yours forever*
Daisy: *innocence*
Daisy (colored): *beauty*
Daisy (Michaelmas): *farewell*
Daisy (white wild): *I will think of it*
Fern: *sincerity*
Forget-me-not: *constancy, true love*
Foxglove: *insincerity, stateliness, youth*
Gardenia: *refinement, secret love*
Hazel: *reconciliation, my heart is agitated*
Hollyhock: *ambition, fruitfulness*
Honeysuckle: *bonds of love*
Hyacinth: *constancy*
Hyacinth (purple): *jealousy, sorrow, forgive me*
Hyacinth (white): *modest loveliness*
Iris: *faith, hope, wisdom, valor*
Jasmine: *I am too happy, amiability*
Lily-of-the-valley: *perfect purity, return of happiness, humility*
Magnolia: *benevolence, magnificence*
Narcissus: *egotism, stay sweet*
Nasturtium: *patriotism, conquest*
Orchid: *you are beautiful, you flatter me, refinement*
Pansy: *modesty, think of me*
Petunia: *you soothe me*
Tulip (red): *I declare my love*
Tulip (variegated): *you enchant me, your eyes are beautiful*
Tulip (yellow): *hopelessness, perfect love*
Violet (blue): *watchfulness, faithfulness*
Violet (white): *let us take a chance*
Wisteria: *cordial welcome* ⌛

OCCULT LONDON

At the end of the 19th century the British Satanist Aleister Crowley, the self-styled "Great Beast," stayed at 67–69 Chancery Lane in London under the alias Count Vladimir Svareff. Later, he lived at 93 Jermyn Street, now better known for tailoring than black masses.

The English architect Nicholas Hawksmoor, former assistant to Sir Christopher Wren and Sir John Vanbrugh, built a series of baroque London churches in the early 18th century. Among his most prominent commissions are St. George's in Bloomsbury, St. Mary Woolnoth in Lombard Street, St. George-in-the-East in Wapping, St. Alfege's in Greenwich, and St. Anne's in Limehouse. It is claimed that if the positions of these churches are mapped, they form a pentacle, and are a significant London occult landmark.

THE SECRET HISTORY OF HITLER'S SKULL

After the fall of Berlin in 1945 and the German surrender, the precise fate of Hitler was still unknown. The British historian Hugh Trevor-Roper (who would later mistakenly authenticate the "Hitler diaries") investigated his final days and concluded that he had committed suicide in the bunker along with Eva Braun. However, the whereabouts of his remains was a continuing puzzle. 55 years after the end of the war, an exhibition mounted in Russia in 2000 promised to reveal the truth. In May 1945, a Red Army team had found the charred corpses of Hitler and his wife of just one day. His staff had burnt the bodies in a shell crater, along with a German shepherd dog and a puppy. The remains were removed by the Soviets and later positively identified by Germans familiar with Hitler's dental work. Stalin ordered that the discovery should be kept secret, thus perpetuating a mystery that lasted for half a century. The skull and a fragment of jaw were removed to Moscow, and the rest of the body buried at an army base in Magdeburg, East Germany. According to Russian sources, they were dug up in 1970, burnt once again and the ashes disposed of in the city sewers.

HOW HARRY HOUDINI DID IT

Harry Houdini was born Ehrich Weiss on 24 March 1874 in Budapest, Hungary. He was undoubtedly the most famous escapologist of all time. To begin with, his feats were relatively simple, involving escaping from handcuffs while in full view of his audience. Later they began to involve immersion in water while being restricted by chains held together by multiple padlocks—this time behind a curtain. It would be wrong to try and uncover all the secret tricks of his trade, but here is a major element of one: when he was chained up, the large padlock he always used could easily be opened and contained keys for all the others.

WINE SECRETS

Some red wine is much better for cardiovascular maintenance than others. The higher the altitude grapes were grown at, the greater the concentration of the sunlight and the relatively higher forming of polyphenols—the substance that prevents artery-hardening. Cabernet or Chianti are particularly profuse in this department.

Moderate alcohol consumption—one or two drinks a day—decreases the likelihood of your developing Type 2 Diabetes. A recent study in the U.S., of 23,000 pairs of twins, showed 40 percent fewer cases of Adult-Onset or Type 2 Diabetes.

Auto passengers who have been drinking are 50 percent more likely to get injured in an accident, and not simply because they're too drunk to manage the seatbelt. Alcohol in the system temporarily weakens cell membranes meaning they are more likely to rupture on impact.

Ice cubes can be stored in the freezer without them sticking together if you keep them in a linen bag. An old linen pillowcase—well washed, of course—is just right for the job.

Smell wine before you taste it. Most of your taste sensations come through smell, and it will save you putting inferior wine in your mouth.

Sediment at the bottom of a bottle of wine can be a very good sign, as it shows the wine hasn't been overly filtered and the remaining particles will have helped it to age and mature.

Remove a stubborn cork from a wine bottle by tightly wrapping the neck in a cloth dipped in boiling water—it will heat up and slightly expand the glass, allowing the cork to move more freely.

Red wine vinegar is red wine gone bad through contact with air, so don't throw red wine away if it has gone bad; keep it and use it as vinegar. It's what restaurants do.

Cheaper sparkling wines are made in exactly the same way as fizzy soft drinks: the carbon dioxide to make it bubble is pumped in at the end of the manufacturing process, just before it is bottled. More expensive sparkling wines or Champagne will be made to sparkle with a second or bottle fermentation—at the bottling stage a precise amount of sugar and yeast is added to the wine to restart the fermentation process and produce carbon dioxide within the liquid; once the pressure in the bottle is released by popping the cork this escapes as streams of tiny bubbles. This is what will be described on the label as "Méthode Traditionelle" or "Méthode

Champagnoise," and because it is the wine itself that continues to produce the gas it will retain its fizz for a long time, often overnight.

The vast majority of wine should be drunk within its first year. Experts say that only the very best 1 percent of all the world's wine production continues to improve after 10 years, and then for no more than 10 years after that. The top 10 percent of all reds and the top 5 percent of all whites improve after a year, but they won't continue to for longer than another 4 years.

The French wine trade has embraced organic viticulture with considerable gusto, in some cases going as far as to employ a system known as Biodynamics. This involves an approach very similar to homeopathic healing, in which relatively tiny amounts of specific natural plant extracts are introduced to the soil. Oh yes, it also measures doses in conjunction with the moon's cycle, but, according to the evidence of the vines, it works.

THE SECRETS OF REMEMBERING

Age is frequently blamed for a failing memory but advancing years are not always the cause. Like all muscles, the brain needs regular exercise or it will become flabby. So regular mental exercises will help. The next time you find yourself at a loss in the grocery store, consider the following.

MAKE AN EFFORT.

If you need to remember something, take notes. Seeing something in writing will get your brain into gear.

CONJURE UP A CLEVER MNEMONIC.

After all, we all remember "Never Eat Shredded Wheat" for the points of a compass. It also helps that this particular mnemonic has the added extra of rhyming, which is another excellent memory tool.

USE THE LINK METHOD.

This ingenious technique is perfect for remembering lists. The theory is that you link each item on the list to the next by way of a story.

THINK VISUALLY.

The majority of people remember things best with a visual picture. Create your own.

HAVE A GOOD NIGHT'S SLEEP.

Countless research has proven that if you are not well rested, your memory will be all over the place.

REPEAT YOURSELF.

Learning a subject parrot-fashion used to be the preferred teaching method in schools, and for good reason. Repetition ingrains on the brain.

EAT WELL.

Supplement your diet with ginkgo biloba, a traditional Chinese medicine extracted from the leaf of the ginkgo plant. And stay away from alcohol—too much booze will make your memory more holey than Swiss cheese.

❀

HOW WWIII WAS AVERTED IN THE 1980S

During the Cold War, the Cuban missile crisis is rightly judged as the closest that the world came to a nuclear conflict between East and West. But in autumn 1983, there was another potential nuclear calamity that remains almost wholly unreported.

In 1981, a seriously ill Leonid Brezhnev convened a special KGB conference, at which he denounced the policies of the new U.S. President, Ronald Reagan. The head of the KGB, Yuri Andropov, who would succeed Brezhnev as general secretary the following year, announced a major Soviet intelligence-gathering initiative.

Codenamed RYAN, an acronym from the Russian for "nuclear missile attack," it would collect information on what were presumed to be western plans for a nuclear strike. Soviet paranoia over the intentions of the Reagan administration was reinforced by the announcement of the U.S. Strategic Defense Initiative, or "Star Wars," by the president on a nationwide television address on 23 March 1983.

This was interpreted by the proponents of RYAN as the first step in preparing the American people for war. The election of Helmut Kohl in West Germany in 1982 and the re-election of Margaret Thatcher in Britain confirmed that Europe would provide a base for American nuclear weapons. The sense of emergency reached a new peak on 1 September, when the Russians shot down the Korean airliner, KAL-007, which had strayed into Soviet airspace after a navigational error.

Andropov, himself now ailing, was using inflammatory language, denouncing the "outrageous military psychosis" of the Reagan administration. The situation reached crisis point when NATO began its exercise "Able Archer 83" in November.

The maneuvers were a practice-run to try out command procedures in the event of nuclear war, but many in the Soviet intelligence establishment feared that they might disguise a first strike attack.

Tension was only diffused when it was realized that the president and the Joint Chiefs of Staff were not involved in the exercise. Although the Soviets remained on high alert until the end of Able Archer, the potential catastrophe of a Russian atomic response was averted.

FLIGHT CONTROL SECRETS #2

Commercial airplanes are so rigorously checked that mechanical or engineering failure now accounts for less than 5 percent of all accidents. Airplanes are checked fully before each flight, and routine checks escalate as flying hours clock up: at 25,000 hours (approximately 5 years) a plane will be stripped right down and rebuilt in a process that takes over a month.

※ ※ ※

Short-haul aircraft are checked far more frequently as they perform relatively more take-offs and landings, and increase and decrease cabin pressure more frequently, all of which puts a great deal of stress on the aircraft.

※ ※ ※

Dulles International Airport in Washington, D.C. was renamed Washington Dulles Airport during the Reagan years because the president kept getting confused between that and Dallas International in Texas, which was renamed Dallas/Fort Worth.

※ ※ ※

Don't complain or make too much fuss at check-in. If you read the small print on your ticket very carefully, you will discover that it doesn't entitle you to be flown anywhere—airlines will always have the final word in disputes with passengers as they are not legally obliged to honor your ticket.

※ ※ ※

Every aircraft in service can be identified by a Hull Number, which is noted on an international register, which keeps a record of service history, repairs, and replaced parts. However, disreputable small airlines are circumventing this procedure through a layer of aircraft traders who buy decommissioned craft for scrap, and sell them back into service without a valid Hull Number. This practice is seen mostly in India and Africa.

※ ※ ※

Apart from mechanical failure, the most common reason flights (both scheduled and charter) are canceled is because of unsold seats. If an airline hasn't sold enough seats for the flight to at least cover its costs the airline will simply cancel it and distribute the passengers elsewhere. This is particularly noticeable on very early morning scheduled flights. 🖫

SECRETS OF THE VOODOO QUEEN

Mary Laveau was the most celebrated Voodoo queen in the world. She lived in 19th-century New Orleans and practiced her supernatural arts with charms, gris-gris (small bags full of herbs and dead matter), snakes, dolls, skulls, and other paraphernalia of sorcery and black magic. Rich and poor would pay for her help, casting hexes or love potions, getting rid of enemies or predicting the future. Now researchers believe that her uncanny knowledge and power base came from a wide network of servants and slaves who, terrified of being hexed by her, spied on their masters and mistresses and reported the information back.

Even more remarkable is that this renowned sorceress rejected her Voodoo faith in later life and ended her days a devout Catholic, visiting local prisons to bring gumbo (New Orleans seafood stew) and solace to those on death row.

THE SECRET OF KEEPING A SECRET

"THREE MAY KEEP A SECRET, IF TWO OF THEM ARE DEAD."
Benjamin Franklin (*18th-century American inventor*)

CHEMICAL WARFARE EXPERIMENTS ON THE NEW YORK SUBWAY

In 1966, the U.S. Army carried out biological warfare experiments on the New York Subway without informing the population. A light bulb filled with a harmless bacterium *Bacillus subtilis* variant *niger* was smashed onto the tracks. Within 20 minutes, it had spread throughout the system and affected a million civilians. Experts estimated that had a more deadly organism been released, thousands of lives would have been at risk.

THE SECRET OF THE WINCHESTER HOUSE

Sarah L. Winchester came into the Winchester Rifle fortune when her husband Willliam died young of tuberculosis in 1881. Their only child, Anna, had died as a baby, and distraught at this second death, Sarah sought help in spiritualism. She was told by a medium that there was a curse on her family and the souls of those killed by her family's gun business would only rest easy if she traveled west and kept building a house for them to live in—if she stopped the building work, she would die. She moved to San Jose, and started work on what came to be called the Winchester Mystery House. This astonishing building was continually changed and extended until her death in 1922, 36 years later. She had carpenters and builders working 24 hours a day and, by the end, there were 160 rooms (including 40 bedrooms), 47 fireplaces, and a number of curious features, such as staircases that lead nowhere and the recurrence of the number 13 in the design.

HITLER'S SECRET INDIAN ARMY

Secret British Intelligence files accessed in 2004 revealed that from 1941, thousands of Indian soldiers fighting for Britain switched their allegiance to Hitler's side. This they did in the belief that he would help remove the British Raj from India, giving the country back its independence.

The attempt was initiated by left-wing revolutionary leader Subhas Chandra Bose who had been arrested by the British in India 11 times. To start with he wanted 500 Indian volunteers to be trained in Germany and then parachuted into India. Thousands volunteered.

Six months after first visiting Germany, Bose had set up the "Free India Center" with the German Foreign Ministry, turning out publicity material, broadcasts, and speeches. To raise a force of 100,000 men, he then began recruiting from German POW camps which housed tens of thousands of Indian soldiers captured by Rommel in North Africa.

In all, 3,000 prisoners of war swore the oath of the "Free India Legion": "I swear by God this holy oath that I will obey the leader of the German race and state, Adolf Hitler, as the commander of the German armed forces in the fight for India, whose leader is Subhas Chandra Bose."

Bose's jubilance was to be short-lived. First his left-wing politics gave him grave concerns about the Germans crossing the Soviet border, then he realized that their retreat would leave little scope for driving the British out of India; in turn it became clear that the Germans' apparent support for his cause was really only Nazi propaganda.

In February 1943, demoralized, he slipped off to Japan—where he recruited a further 60,000 men to his cause—leaving his Free India legionaries rudderless and demoralized. Before long the Indian forces had gained a bad reputation among the civilians of the countries they occupied. One ex-French Resistance fighter recalled cases of rape and the shooting of a young girl as they passed through his hometown, Ruffec.

The Indian legionnaires were sent back to India after the war, where they all served short jail sentences and were then released. The British Raj recognized that its time had come to an end, that the Indian army was not wholly within its grasp, and Indian independence followed. Too late for Subhas Chandra Bose, though, who had died in 1945. ⌛

THE DIRTY SECRET OF IVORY SOAP

In 1972, the Ivory Snow box featured a picture of a mother and baby. The mother—not the baby as some have claimed—went on to be a porn star: Marilyn Chambers, who starred in the classic *Behind the Green Door*. It is even said that each of her films features a reference to Ivory Snow . . .

THE SECRETS OF PENNY LANE

Underneath the Edge Hill area of Liverpool, England, is an extraordinary labyrinth of tunnels built in the 19th century on the orders of a local millionaire. Joseph Williamson, who had made his fortune from tobacco, was moved by the poverty and widespread unemployment of soldiers returning from the Napoleonic wars. As a job creation scheme, he cooked up a plan to provide employment by building a network of tunnels. Work started in 1816, and for the next 20 years provided work for laborers, masons, joiners, and bricklayers. One tunnel was built so that Williamson and his wife could go to church without getting wet, another was designed as an underground room where he could lavish subterranean hospitality on his friends, while others were simply dead ends. On one occasion members of Williamson's tunneling gang came across the workers of the legendary engineer Robert Stephenson, who were building a railway tunnel. When Stephenson saw the quality of their craftsmanship, he invited them to come and work for him. As Williamson grew older, he became increasingly reclusive, spending his last few years alone in his underground kingdom. He lives on in Liverpool folklore as the Mad Mole of Edge Hill.

THE SUPER SIZE SECRET

Between the years 2000 and 2005, portions in popular restaurants and of pre-packaged food grew progressively larger—in restaurants across the board, they were one-third bigger in 2005 than they were 5 years before. Unbelievably, this was a strategy arrived at by the food industries in order to increase profits as they couldn't charge any more for food without appearing to give better value.

The secret of how they managed to make it look as if the customer was getting more for their money, while taking more money from the customer is this: The cheaper ingredients and foods—specifically the carbohydrates—were increased out of proportion to the dish itself, meaning a burger or pizza that seemed, for instance, 30 percent bigger only had its manufacturing costs increased by around 10 percent. It also means that the caloric values shot up: between 2000 and '05, the caloric content of the average portion of large fries—taken across several well-known fast food outlets—more than doubled from 250 to 600 calories.

This not only vastly hiked the mark-up on processed and mass-produced food, but the perpetual inflating of portion sizes changed the way many people approached buying food, first in restaurants and then in the supermarket. When faced with the apparent value of a jumbo-sized meal, it didn't take long for people to accept these new servings to the point that what used to seem satisfactory suddenly looked positively puny. Restaurant plates got bigger, takeaway cartons subtly increased in size. Then food items got resized on the menu, notably with chocolate bars and pizzas: what was large is now medium and a new size has been added on top. Yet because people are more often than not programmed from childhood to finish what's put in front of them they still eat it all. And still feel hungry after at much the same time as they always have because so much of this new huge meal consists of empty calories, hence they eat another big meal.

THE SECRET WWII ALLIED WEAPON

Jasper Maskelyne was a third-generation stage magician, and already a major star in pre-war Britain. At the outbreak of hostilities in 1939 he joined the Royal Engineers, hoping that his skills as an illusionist could be put to use. Although his initial role was limited to entertaining the troops, he was soon given the opportunity to join a British unit in North Africa known as "A-Force" that had been set up to confuse and deceive the enemy. Maskelyne led a maverick group of artists, carpenters, and criminals, using ingenious and unorthodox methods to hide British positions and create plausible diversions. Dummy tanks were made out of wood and canvas, while the real ones were disguised as trucks. He built a diversionary harbor a few miles up the coast from Alexandria, and even managed to "hide" the Suez Canal from German bombers with the use of revolving mirrors and searchlights. Before the crucial battle of El Alamein in 1942, he created a vast illusion of British forces 30 miles south of their actual position. 2,000 fake tanks were built, supplied by a fake railway line and a half-assembled water pipeline, suggesting that the assault could only begin when it was completed.

The actual battle proved to be a turning point in the war. Churchill wrote in 1951 in his history of the conflict that "Before Alamein we never had a victory. After Alamein we never had a defeat." At the time he praised the "marvelous system of camouflage" in the House of Commons. Despite his undoubted contribution to the war effort, Jasper Maskelyne never received an honor or official recognition for his illusionist work.

ABANDONED NEW YORK SUBWAY STATIONS #9

WORTH STREET

LOCATION: WORTH STREET AND LEONARD STREET BETWEEN
BROOKLYN BRIDGE AND CANAL STREET
OPENED OCTOBER 1904, CLOSED 1962.

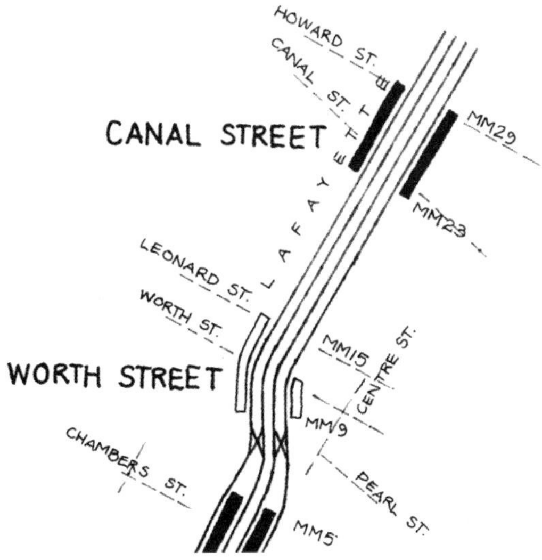

A shallow station with fare controls on each of its two platforms, the most striking thing about the Worth Street station was its rounded rectangle exit on the downtown side. Internally it looks much the same as those in use at Spring Street or Canal Street. The platforms were originally built at a length of 200 feet. This was extended in 1910 and again in 1948 because of new trains and safety regulations, although only one platform (downtown) was extended in the second extension to save costs. When the New York Transit Authority decided in 1956 to extend all stations to a ten-car length, Brooklyn Bridge station was extended so that it came within a block of the Worth Street entrance and was renamed Brooklyn Bridge-Worth Street. The original station was closed.

THE COLONEL'S SECRET

Although the actual KFC recipe remains locked in a vault somewhere, probably in deepest Kentucky and guarded by large men in cowboy hats, follow the instructions below and your fried chicken will be indistinguishable from the Colonel's finest.

EQUIPMENT:

Two large mixing bowls
A whisk
Large cook's knife and chopping board
A tray for rolling chicken pieces in flour
A deep fat fryer, corn oil, and thermometer

INGREDIENTS:

1 chicken cut into eight pieces for frying (2 × breast, wing, thigh, drumstick)
2 eggs
½ cup milk
⅔ cup flour (half plain/half self-raising)
4oz fine fresh breadcrumbs (make your own, don't open a packet!)
1 Knorr chicken stock cube
½ teaspoon garlic powder (not garlic salt, but dried powdered garlic)
½ teaspoon onion powder (not onion salt . . .)
½ teaspoon paprika
1 tablespoon finely chopped fresh parsley
2 large cloves garlic
½ teaspoon salt
½ teaspoon soy sauce
½ teaspoon Worcestershire sauce
2 teaspoons black peppercorns

METHOD:

In one of the mixing bowls, thoroughly beat eggs, milk, soy sauce, and Worcestershire sauce together.

Using the flat of the knife and a corner of the chopping board, grind garlic into a paste with the salt and beat into mixture.

Add half the parsley, the crumbled stock cube, and about a quarter of the flour.

Beat in thoroughly to avoid any lumps.

Separate about half the remaining flour onto the tray for rolling the chicken pieces.

In the second mixing bowl, thoroughly combine the other half of the flour and the breadcrumbs.

Crush the peppercorns on the chopping board under the heel of the knife and add to flour.

Blend in the rest of the ingredients, mixing together well with your fingers.

Heat oil in deep fat fryer to 360 degrees F. (Oil temperature is crucial, as too hot oil will burn the coating before the chicken inside is fully cooked, while too cool will mean the crumbs and flour absorb the oil to become soggy.)

Roll each piece of chicken in the flour on the tray until thoroughly coated. (If the flour starts to run out before you have finished coating your chicken, simply top the tray up with extra plain flour.)

Immerse into the egg and milk mixture in the first mixing bowl.

Roll in the flour/breadcrumbs bowl until totally coated.

Lower gently into the hot oil and fry until golden brown in color—3 or 4 minutes approximately.

Remove from oil and drain on a tray covered in paper towels.

Or—alternative finish—serve in a thin cardboard box that soaks up the surplus oil and subsequently transfers it to your clothes. 🖫

PRE-20TH-CENTURY BRITISH EXECUTIONERS AND THEIR FAMOUS VICTIMS

The identity of British executioners was always kept a secret in order to protect the man and his family from suffering revenge attacks from the families of people he killed.

RICHARD BRANDON,
AKA GREGORY

CROWN EXECUTIONER 1640–1649

Inherited the position from his father, Richard.

Famous victims: Sir Thomas Wentworth, the Earl of Strafford in 1641. Archbishop of Canterbury William Laud in 1644.

JACK KETCH

CROWN EXECUTIONER 1663–1686

The most feared yet incompetent executioner of his age. Most feared for the length of time that he served in the office, most incompetent because despite practice he could take several blows to succeed.

Famous victim: Lord William Russell in July 1683. Ketch was given 10 guineas to do his job swiftly. After the first blow Lord Russell cursed Ketch for failure. It took three more before the head was severed. Ketch's name is still evoked today in the British Punch and Judy puppet show as that of the hangman.

JOHN THRIFT

CROWN EXECUTIONER 1747

Famous victim: Lord Lovat, the last man to be beheaded in England. The 70-year- d Earl handed Thrift 10 guineas and asked to see the axe. After examining it, Lovat declared that it would do. Thrift took one blow to sever Lovat's head from his body.

THOMAS TURLIS

CROWN EXECUTIONER 1760

Famous victim: Earl Ferrers, the only peer to be hanged for murder. Ferrers defended himself in court using a plea of insanity after the killing of one of his servants.

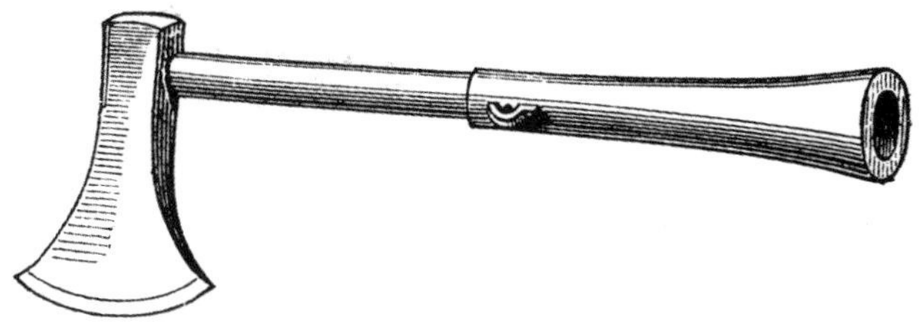

WILLIAM CALCRAFT

CROWN EXECUTIONER 1829–1874

He was the last salaried official executioner in England. Calcraft was the official executioner at Newgate Prison (where he also performed floggings), Horsemonger Lane Gaol in Surrey, and Maidstone Prison. He would be paid between £10 and £15 per hanging and received 1 guinea a week as a retainer from Newgate, who paid him another guinea per execution and half a crown for each flogging. He was allowed to sell the personal effects of his victims. His more infamous victims belongings would often end up at Madame Tussaud's Waxworks.

Famous victims: Francis Kidder, the last publicly executed woman in the country on 2 April 1868 (for drowning her stepdaughter).

Michael Barrett, the last publicly executed man on 26 May 1868 (he was an IRA bomber who killed 12 people with one explosion).

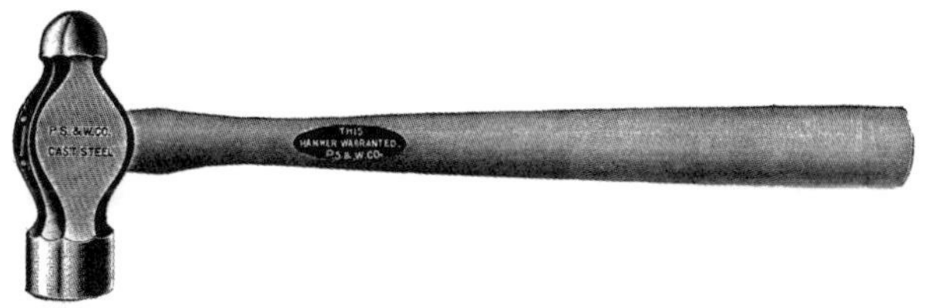

CHINESE BANK PROPAGANDA

During WWII, the Japanese took over the running of the banks in collaborationist China. But Chinese bank staff managed to get a message of resistance and hope to their people by means of clever propaganda. On some 1940 Central Reserve Bank of China notes, the English letters C G W S R can clearly be seen, perhaps standing for "Central Government Will Soon Return," a popular catchphrase of the time. The 1944 200-yuan notes contain the letters U S A C, which are thought to mean "United States Army Coming." Other banknotes were stamped with ink propaganda slogans such as "Resist the Japanese, rebuild the nation" while in circulation.

LONDON'S SECRET WATTS MEMORIAL

The Watts Memorial in Postman's Park, not far from St. Paul's Cathedral in London, is perhaps London's most unusual hidden monument. The painter and sculptor George Frederick Watts had proposed that Queen Victoria's Golden Jubilee in 1887 be marked with a memorial to the heroism of ordinary people—a tribute to the kindness of strangers. But officialdom wasn't interested in such a quirky project and so the egalitarian Watts funded it himself. The Watts Memorial is an open-air loggia-type gallery set in the quiet oasis of this small park. On the wall, inscribed glazed-tile panels simply tell the stories of individual acts of personal bravery that tragically ended in the loss of the heroic person's life. Originally there were only 13 inscriptions but Watts's widow Mary added more after his death. The inscriptions are brief and moving, for example:

"Sarah Smith, pantomime artist. At Prince's Theatre died of terrible injuries received when attempting in her inflammable dress to extinguish the flames which had enveloped her companion. January 24 1863."

"John Clinton, aged 10, who was drowned near London Bridge in trying to save a companion younger than himself. July 16 1894."

THE REAL BEVERLY HILLBILLIES

The elite Beverly Hills High School at 241 Moreno Drive is the site of a functioning oil derrick. The operation is carefully managed so as to minimize disruption to pupils, but still produces around 600 barrels of oil a day and thousands of dollars a month in revenues for the school and the local community.

THE ROLLING STONES'S SWEET SECRET

By 1969 the Rolling Stones were at the very top of their game. That year, on their triumphant American comeback tour, they were routinely—and quite justifiably—introduced as "the greatest rock & roll band in the world." Meanwhile, however, The Beatles had been cloistered at Abbey Road, relentlessly upping the ante with their audacious approach to album production and cover art; off the road, the Stones now lagged a long way behind. The band's 1968 *Beggars Banquet* was superb, but lingered in the vaults for nearly a year because the record label objected to the Stones's chosen cover, which had been a shot of the graffiti-scarred toilet wall in a Mexican restaurant in LA.

Let It Bleed would be different: the album boasted a clutch of future Stones classics including "Gimme Shelter," "Midnight Rambler," and "You Can't Always Get What You Want," which the band wanted heard as soon as possible. So, this time around, the cover had to be innocuous. For no obvious reason, a cake appeared on the front and back sleeves, perched on top of a tape reel and a tire. 5 tiny figures representing the Stones were balanced on top of the cake. The creator of what *Mojo* magazine called "the most celebrated sponge cake in rock" was a 26-year-old home economist called Delia Smith. The British queen of plain cooking was yet to make her TV debut, but was clearly mixing with the right crowd. The Stones later autographed the cover for her, and that copy now hangs in the restaurant at the world-famous cook's beloved Norwich City soccer ground.

FOOD STUFF THEY'D RATHER YOU DIDN'T KNOW #2

Apart from the price and, obviously, the color there is no difference between brown and white eggs. What is inside the shell is exactly the same, why they look different is because white eggs come from the more prevalent white-feathered hens, and brown eggs come from the less-common red feathered variety.

Fresh TV dinners contain far more preservatives than their frozen counterparts.

Not all low-fat spreads are suitable for vegetarians, as the lower the fat content the more likely the spread is to require a setting agent to hold it firm, and the most commonly used is gelatine. Read the labels carefully.

Nut allergies appear to be on the rise because so many products have ground nuts in them now as a cheap bulking agent.

The chemicals in the most commonly used pesticides have been linked with declining sperm counts and rising rates of breast cancer.

The earliest recorded example of food additives came in the 15th century when unscrupulous merchants were mixing gravel and bits of bark in with the pepper they were selling.

Vanilla flavoring is a by-product of the petroleum industry, vanilla essence is extracted from vanilla plants.

Unsalted butter will usually be better quality, as manufacturers are aware that the salt will mask all sorts of flavoring imperfections.

By law, food labels cannot feature pictures of items they don't contain: if a yogurt has a picture of a raspberry on the pot then there has to be some real raspberry content.

AMERICAN PIE SECRETS

Don McLean's "American Pie" reached #2 in Britain in January 1972. At 8 minutes 27 seconds long, it was inspired by the events of 3 February 1959—"the day the music died"—when the plane carrying Buddy Holly, Ritchie Valens, and The Big Bopper crashed into a snowy field, killing everyone on board. McLean's lyrics also referenced Mick Jagger at Altamont ("Satan laughing with delight"), Bob Dylan ("the jester on the sideline in a cast"), and The Beatles ("the quartet practiced in the park"). "American Pie" was written in a single day and the hit version was recorded in just one take. In 1991 Don McLean copyrighted the phrase "American Pie," and he protects it jealously—the makers of the movie *American Pie* had to ask permission to use the title. At the start of the new millennium, this most personal of songs was given a radical makeover when Madonna's cover version reached #1. What does "American Pie" mean to McLean now? "It means," he says, "that I don't have to work if I don't want to."

THE SECRET HISTORY OF GUNPOWDER

The popular belief that the Chinese discovered gunpowder is vehemently disputed in many circles, notably in the Middle East and the Indian subcontinent, where it is thought that the Moors developed explosives a few hundred years earlier. Apparently, the reason European historians credit the Chinese is because gunpowder arrived in Europe from China courtesy of Marco Polo in the 13th century.

The Moors and the Indians were certainly the first to exploit the weapons potential of gunpowder. The Chinese had the material for several hundred years before they considered making cannons or guns—it had no weapons usage when Marco Polo brought it back. The Moors were recorded using cannon in battle as early as the 12th century.

THE SECRET OF SUCCESSFUL PARENTING

"PARENTS CAN ONLY ADVISE THEIR CHILDREN OR POINT THEM IN THE RIGHT DIRECTION. ULTIMATELY PEOPLE SHAPE THEIR OWN CHARACTERS."
Anne Frank (*20th-century Dutch diarist*)

"THERE ARE TIMES WHEN PARENTHOOD SEEMS NOTHING BUT FEEDING THE MOUTH THAT BITES YOU."
Peter De Vries (*20th-century American author*)

"CHILDREN AREN'T HAPPY WITHOUT SOMETHING TO IGNORE, AND THAT'S WHAT PARENTS WERE CREATED FOR."
Ogden Nash (*20th-century American poet*)

"I HAVE FOUND THE BEST WAY TO GIVE ADVICE TO YOUR CHILDREN IS TO FIND OUT WHAT THEY WANT AND THEN ADVISE THEM TO DO IT."
Harry S. Truman (*20th-century American president*)

THE SECRETS OF SUCCESSFULLY SELLING YOUR HOUSE

Choose the time of year to sell that best suits your house. If you have a well-stocked, flowering garden for instance, show the house at the height of its flowering. If you have a cosy place that is best shown in the light of a glowing fire, show it in early winter, pre-Christmas. If your swimming pool is a major asset, sell in early summer (but keep people out of the pool while showing).

Try to recall when you bought the house and what attracted you to it—chances are the same things will attract a new buyer. Enhance those features.

First impressions count. Tidy the front yard, give the front door a fresh lick of paint and de-clutter the entrance hall. You may even need to go as far as sweeping public areas like the sidewalk in front of your house—many buyers make their decision on the curb appeal of a property.

Make sure that every room in your house is clean and tidy.

Think about creating a home, not just a house. Buyers want an environment that feels warm. Imagine your potential buyer and market your house accordingly.

Tidy up. It may sound obvious, but unsightly mess doesn't only refer to any unwashed dishes (an obvious no-no) but also to too much clutter. Hide as much as you can from view to create a free-flowing environment.

Get rid of pets. Lots of people don't like them and they can be rather, well, smelly. The same goes for children and their paraphernalia, too.

Bake some bread—yes, this really does work! As does the similarly enticing aroma of freshly brewed coffee. Fresh flowers will also make your house seem more inviting to potential buyers.

Erase anything too "individual" from clear view. Many buyers have firm ideas about how an interior should look and have a difficult time seeing past what, to them, is a mistake. To be absolutely sure that your interior won't upset anyone, it's worth spending a small amount of money on painting your walls in neutral shades.

Bathrooms and kitchens sell houses so make sure yours are extra-special. Re-tile and re-fit if necessary—the cost of any extra work will be recouped when you sell your home. After all, the last thing you want is a house listed as "needing work."

Market any outside space as an extra room. In other words, add tables, chairs, and seductive lighting.

Lighten up. Put on as many lights and lamps as possible when showing potential buyers around. A dark corner can be a distinct disadvantage when showing a home. Make sure your windows are washed, both inside and out. ❀

SECRETS OF THE DARK SIDE OF THE MOON

Pink Floyd's *Dark Side Of The Moon* is the best-selling album ever released by a British band. Since 1973, the album has sold an estimated 30 million copies worldwide. If *Dark Side Of The Moon* were a country, it would be Canada. But the album had propelled the Floyd from being a cult "underground" band into a stadium-filling, headlining act. And they weren't quite sure what to do next.

As ever in rock & roll, a follow-up album was needed to consolidate their success. But the Floyd, notoriously painstaking at the best of times, were intimidated by the expectations of their next album. In the end, they decided to follow-up *Dark Side Of The Moon* with . . . *Household Objects*. But you needn't search for a review; *Household Objects* never made it beyond the walls of the Abbey Road studios.

The aim was to make an album—but *without* using musical instruments. The Floyd's Roger Waters remembered: "There was a lot of going into the studio and chopping wood . . . And you'd spend weeks and weeks recording a rubber band . . . Weeks and weeks of wasting time."

"We unrolled lengths of adhesive tape, sprayed aerosols, plucked egg slicers and tapped wine bottle tops," recalled drummer Nick Mason. "After a number of weeks, musical progress was negligible . . . and the whole project was gently laid to rest." But undeterred, Pink Floyd went back to their musical instruments, and their 1975 album *Wish You Were Here* became the #1 album in Britain and America.

SECRETS OF SUVEILLANCE

With the advent of the internet came a new source of government intelligence gathering hardware. Possibly the largest and most awe-inpiring invention is ECHELON, a massive computer system that monitors every piece of electronic information that is broadcast or sent over the internet, anywhere in the world. Stations housing ECHELON hardware are situated around the globe and the information that it gathers is shared between American and British intelligence services.

The surveillance system is progammed to identify key words in emails and on web sites, intercept the whole message or content and file away to be further analyzed by intelligence agents. If there is anyone who might doubt the existence of such a machine or that it could not be used in the West, they should read the following.

It is taken from a July 2001 Report of the European Parliament on the existence of a global system for the interception of private and commercial communications (ECHELON interception system).

> *(W)hereas the existence of a global system for intercepting communications, operating by means of co-operation proportionate to their capabilities among the USA, the UK, Canada, Australia and New Zealand under the UKUSA Agreement, is no longer in doubt; it seems likely, in view of the evidence and the consistent pattern of statements from a very wide range of individuals and organizations, including American sources, that its name is in fact ECHELON.*
>
> Plus, *"the interception of communications is a method of spying commonly employed by intelligence services, so that other states might also operate similar systems, provided that they have the required funds and the right locations. France is the only EU Member State which is—thanks to its overseas territories—geographically and technically capable of operating autonomously a global interception system and also possesses the technical and organizational infrastructure to do so. There is also ample evidence that Russia is likely to operate such a system."*

So if you were wondering why certain emails that you'd sent were not getting to their intended recipient, take a look at the language of your message and remove any possibly "dangerous" words, such as "bomb," "conspiracy," "fatwah," or "Cheney." Re-send and then you'll find the message makes it to its destination. But be prepared for a loud knock on your front door at a very early time of the morning, soon.

ROMAN FACE CREAM

In the Tabard Square archaeological ruins in London's Southwark, the remains of the oldest-known cosmetic face cream was excavated in 2003. A small metal canister was found in a drain on the site of a Romano-Celtic temple, and has been dated to the 2nd century A.D. The pot contained a thick white cream with fingermarks inside the lid, presumably those of the Roman lady to whom it belonged. The cream was analyzed and found to contain lead oxide, which whitens the skin, as well as animal fats and starch, to moisturize it. The site is now being developed to provide shops and houses.

THE SECRET CHICKEN OF DOWNING STREET

The prime minister of Great Britain lives at number 10 Downing Street in London. The building has been home to the head of the British government since the 18th century, when the last private resident to live there rejoiced in the name of Mr. Chicken (he left in 1735). The street was built at the end of the 17th century by Lord Downing, a former spy for Oliver Cromwell during the English Civil War who switched allegiance after the Roundhead leader died in 1658. What is now number 10 Downing Street was originally number 5. What's less known is that, despite the armed guards and security gates permanently situated at the end of the street, the road is still a public right of way. Politely insist and you will be allowed to walk along Downing Street, albeit with an armed escort.

NEW ORLEANS'S SECRET BURIAL PIT

Located at 1140 Royal Street in New Orleans, and owned in the 1830s by a Dr. Lalaurie and his wife, Delphine, this mansion developed a dark reputation. Slaves seemed to disappear regularly from the household, and the family said they'd escaped or been sold on. Rumors started when Madame Lalaurie was seen chasing a servant girl with a whip, who jumped to her death from a window rather than be caught by her mistress. Still, it wasn't until the house caught fire in 1834 that the full horrors in the Lalaurie mansion were revealed. In the attic, firefighters found slaves who'd been chained and appalingly tortured, with parts of their bodies cut off or mutilated. One woman's mouth had been filled with offal and sewn up, another had her limbs so badly broken she couldn't move, another her stomach cut open and her intestines wrapped as a belt around her waist, while one man had a stick protruding from his head which had apparently been used to stir his brains.

The Lalauries fled immediately after the fire, and the inside of the house was devastated by a furious mob. For 100 years, the building passed from owner to owner, along with rumors of ghosts and poltergeists meant to be the spirits of the people who'd been butchered by the Lalauries. Nobody knew what happened to the couple, or how many slaves they had tortured and killed.

Then in the 1940s, their secrets were uncovered. The then owner of the house was refurbishing the place for resale and workmen dug down under the wooden floors. There they found a hidden burial pit piled full of haphazardly arranged bodies with broken bones. It became clear that this macabre site was where the Lalauries had thrown the dead bodies of the slaves they'd tortured and killed over the years. They had created their own private cemetery beneath the floors of their luxury mansion.

THE TREEHOPPER'S SURVIVAL SECRET

Thorn treehoppers live longer because they live on branches. You see, if it weren't for the telltale sign of six little legs peeping out from under their bodies and clinging tenaciously to a branch or twig, the casual or even more careful observer would take them for thorns. Able to fool their enemies with ease, they lead enjoyable and stress-free lives feeding on sap.

ABANDONED NEW YORK SUBWAY STATIONS #10

CORTLANDT STREET

LOCATION: CORTLANDT STREET BETWEEN PARK PLACE AND RECTOR STREET

OPENED IN JULY 1918, CLOSED SEPTEMBER 2001.

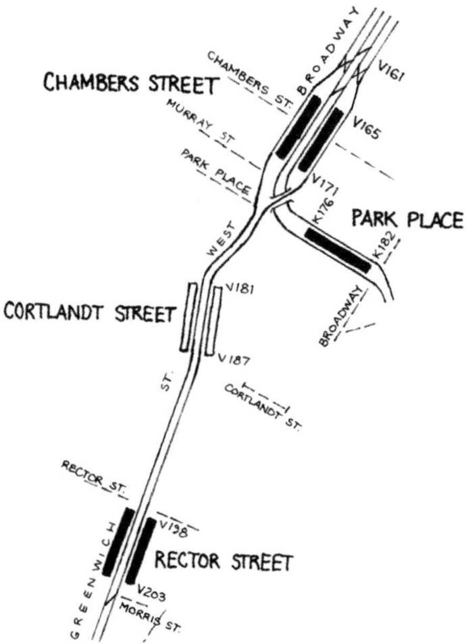

Originally part of the Dual System the station had only two tracks and was built under the oldest part of the city. During its construction, cannonballs and the burned remains of a ship sunk during colonial times were discovered. Extended to the full ten-car length in 1966, it was fully renovated between 1972 and 1976 and renamed Cortlandt Street-World Trade Center when the twin towers opened. The events of 11 September 2001 saw Cortland Street station completely demolished, the first NY Subway station to suffer such a fate. It will be rebuilt and re-opened along with the site.

SECRETS OF WEIGHT LOSS

It takes the brain about 20 minutes to register that the stomach is full, so because we tend to eat much quicker these days, we will overeat—literally—by going past capacity without the brain realizing. Thus a good way to lose weight is simply to eat slower.

※ ※ ※

Drastically cutting the calories is far from the most efficient, or even the most successful, way to lose weight. If you reduce your caloric intake to much below what your body needs (and everybody's body has different needs) it will go into "starvation mode" and readjust your metabolism to burn what you are consuming more slowly and still store some as fat for vital functions or emergencies.

※ ※ ※

People who experience the least weight gain in middle age are likely to have a much happier old age. This isn't simply because of the better health aspect, but test studies carried out in Sweden have shown a much higher level of emotional and spiritual well-being too.

※ ※ ※

We ought to eat five small meals a day rather than three, or less, huge ones—you wouldn't run your car until the tank was bone dry and then fill it to the point that gas was slopping out over your shoes, would you?

※ ※ ※

Eating yogurt will actually help you lose weight, as the high calcium content provides a catalyst for your body to burn fat more efficiently and will actually limit the amount of fat your body will support.

※ ※ ※

White poultry meat will contain roughly half the intrinsic fat of dark meat. The dark meat (the legs) is made from slow twitch muscle fibers of the type used for persistent activities such as walking, while the breast is fast twitch muscle for sudden, occasional movements, and the former requires a greater store of fat to function efficiently.

※ ※ ※

Margarine or vegetable oil spreads have to have less than 65 percent fat to be allowed to call themselves "reduced fat" and 40 percent or less to bear the name "low fat."

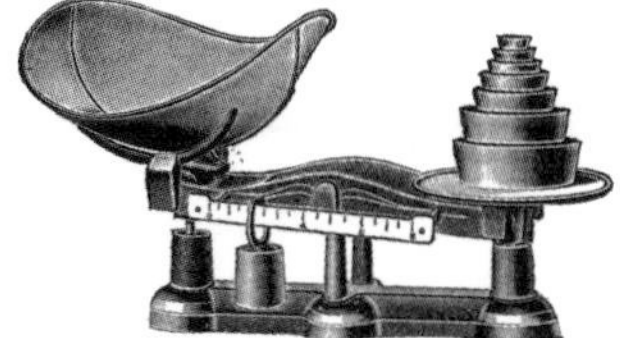

LONDON'S CENTERS OF ESPIONAGE

THAMES HOUSE, MILBANK, SW1.
Current headquarters of MI5 (Security Service).

EUSTON TOWER, NW1.
Center for MI5's "Watcher" surveillance service.

140 GOWER STREET, WC1.
MI5 Headquarters 1976–1995.

VAUXHALL CROSS, SE1.
Headquarters of MI6 (Secret Intelligence Service).

NEW SCOTLAND YARD, SW1, LONDON.
Headquarters of the Special Branch.

THE SECRET TO PERFECTING PASTRY

Pastry is called pastry because it evolved from a flour and water paste that was applied to meat before roasting to seal in the juices. It was inedible and would be discarded before serving.

When baking choux pastry, splash a handful of water on the tray just before it goes in the oven. This will provide just enough steam to help the choux rise.

If overkneaded or over-rolled, pastry will shrink. Once mixed, allow it to rest in the fridge or the freezer for half an hour, then when rolled put it back for another half hour before baking.

When kneading pastry, keep hands cold by plunging them into ice water. It will stop the pastry warming up and softening, then stretching when rolled, and then shrinking back in the oven.

THE SECRETS OF USING A FAN

There is plenty of documentary evidence to show that a Victorian flower code existed, but exactly how formal a fan code there was is open to debate. Some commentators speculate that the "language of fans" was in reality merely an extension of the attitude of a lady toward her would-be suitor. Hence she might flutter her fan flirtatiously, waft it laconically, or even snap it shut in a clear, dismissive "let that be an end to the matter" gesture. Others maintain that it was a much more formal business: that the speed with which the lady used her fan was highly significant, denoting anger, frustration, even love.

Those who take this view to its most extreme believe the language was very specific indeed. The following are a few of the messages that they claim were conveyed:

Resting the fan on the right cheek
yes

Resting the fan on the left cheek
no

Twirling the fan with the left hand
we are being watched

Carrying the fan in front of the face with the right hand *follow me* ⌛

DOUBLE SECRET AGENT REVEALED

In the last years of the Cold War, Aldrich Ames was probably the most successful Soviet agent within the U.S.A. He worked in counter-espionage at the CIA, but from 1985 was also a double agent and betrayed much of the American intelligence operation within the U.S.S.R. At least 10 Russian agents were executed on his information, including Dmitri Polyakov, who had spied for the U.S. since the early 1960s. Ames's motive was financial rather than ideological and he received nearly $3 million for his efforts. He lived at 2512 N. Randolph Street, in Arlington, and would communicate with his Russian handlers by placing chalk marks on a mailbox at 37th and R Streets. 👓

LITTLE KNOWN CULINARY CURIOS #6

To stop icing setting too hard, add either a teaspoon of baking powder to the sugar or a teaspoon of glycerine (available at most drugstores) during the mixing process—it will allow the icing to set hard, but will keep it crumbly.

Contrary to popular belief, you can freeze mushrooms without cooking them first. Sliced, quartered, or whole, once they are cooked there will be very little difference in flavor and texture between thawed out, frozen, and fresh mushrooms.

When making tea, don't let the water boil for too long as the bubbling de-oxygenates the water and the tea won't taste as light and refreshing. For the same reason, don't reboil water, always fill the kettle with fresh water.

ROSEBUD'S SECRET IDENTITY

Orson Welles's 1941 classic *Citizen Kane* is regularly voted the greatest film ever made. It was Welles's first film, but the 25-year old had gone to Hollywood intending to make a film of Joseph Conrad's *Heart Of Darkness*, the novella which, 38 years later, Francis Ford Coppola used as the basis for *Apocalypse Now*.

From the very beginning, the references to "Rosebud" baffled viewers. It was the very first word uttered in the film, and is used repeatedly to try and unravel the enigma of the film's central character, the media mogul, Charles Foster Kane (based on the real-life tycoon William Randolph Hearst). The film's last line confirms the enigma: "I guess Rosebud is just a piece in a jigsaw puzzle, a missing piece."

For years, film historians and critics battled over the symbolism of "Rosebud." There was even one scurrilous suggestion that Welles had somehow discovered Hearst's pet-name for his mistress's hidden charms. Over the years, Welles deftly stoked the fire of the mystery, although he was quite explicit at the time of the film's opening: "Rosebud is the trade name of a cheap sled on which Kane was playing on the day he was taken away from his home and his mother. In his subconscious it represented the simplicity, the comfort, above all the lack of responsibility in his home, and also it stood for his mother's love, which Kane never lost."

THE SECRET OF MAKING A GOOD FIRST IMPRESSION

There is a secret to making a good first impression that has nothing to do with your personality, appearance, or natural ability to charm. The single most important factor is to focus on the other person then incorporate the following four elements into the interaction.

First, make them feel liked and appreciated by directly or indirectly showing you understand and respect them. You could say, for example: "What an interesting idea, I've never thought of it that way before . . ."

Second, establish rapport by showing you have shared interests or areas of connection with them. For example, "Oh yes, I loved that book too, and especially the character of . . ."

Third, stimulate their curiosity and interest by giving them some new and relevant information. For example, to your hairdresser: "I was reading yesterday about Voodoo queen Mary Laveau (see page 129 above), did you know she started out cutting the hair of the aristocracy . . ."

Fourth, lighten other people's mood by being playful and humorous. Never walk into a meeting and complain about your terrible journey, or how bad you feel. Stay positive: you don't need to be a comedian, just ratchet your style upbeat a little.

By following these four secret rules, you will have fulfilled all the needs of the other person, which is what first impressions are actually all about.

THE SECRET OF EXISTENCE

"FOR BELIEVE ME: THE SECRET FOR HARVESTING FROM EXISTENCE THE GREATEST FRUITFULNESS AND GREATEST ENJOYMENT IS—TO LIVE DANGEROUSLY."

Friedrich Nietzsche (*19th-century German philosopher*)

INDEX

AUTHORS

LLOYD BRADLEY

THOMAS EATON

EMMA HOOLEY

PATRICK HUMPHRIES

CHARLOTTE WILLIAMSON